Best Easy Day Hikes
Great Smoky Mountains
National Park

Help Us Keep This Guide Up to Date

Every effort has been made by the author and editors to make this guide as accurate and useful as possible. However, many things can change after a guide is published—trails are rerouted, regulations change, facilities come under new management, etc.

We would love to hear from you concerning your experiences with this guide and how you feel it could be improved and kept up to date. While we may not be able to respond to all comments and suggestions, we'll take them to heart and we'll also make certain to share them with the author. Please send your comments and suggestions to the following address:

Globe Pequot Press
Reader Response/Editorial Department
P.O. Box 480
Guilford, CT 06437

Or you may e-mail us at:

editorial@GlobePequot.com

Thanks for your input, and happy trails!

Best Easy Day Hikes Series

Best Easy Day Hikes
Great Smoky Mountains
National Park

Randy Johnson

FALCONGUIDES

GUILFORD, CONNECTICUT
HELENA, MONTANA
AN IMPRINT OF GLOBE PEQUOT PRESS

FALCONGUIDES®

Project editor: Gregory Hyman
Layout: Kevin Mak
Maps: Hartdale Maps © Morris Book Publishing, LLC

TOPO! Explorer software and SuperQuad source maps courtesy of National Geographic Maps. For information about TOPO! Explorer, TOPO!, and Nat Geo Maps products, go to www.topo.com or www.natgeomaps.com.

Library of Congress Cataloging-in-Publication Data is available on file.

ISBN 978-0-7627-4836-5

Printed in the United States of America

10 9 8 7 6 5 4 3 2 1

Contents

Overview

Northwest Section

Introduction

Great Smoky Mountains is the country's most popular national park. That distinction is due to much more than just proximity to nearby urban areas. This United Nations–designated International Biosphere Reserve—one of the most diverse ecosystems on Earth—is a temperate rainforest that's world-class lush. Despite extensive logging in the early 1900s, 35 percent of the park was never logged, so large tracts of towering virgin timber remain. The 800 square miles of the Smokies is one of the largest intact natural areas in the eastern United States. For the serious explorer, the Smokies contain entire watersheds of peaks and valleys completely devoid of trails. Though motorists rarely see it, hikers can delve into that inspiring wilderness on even short walks.

Ecosystems and Weather

A huge area of the park soars above 4,500 feet to more than 6,600 feet, where cool summers and deep-snow winters prevail in the spruce-fir ecosystem of the Canadian forest zone (comprised of red spruce and Fraser fir). Vast portions of the park also sprawl below 2,500 feet, where a diverse pine and oak forest reigns and summer can bring sticky, even hot weather. Between these two ecosystems, elevation and aspect (the location of the land in damp valley or on dry ridge, on the sunny side or in the shade) yield woodlands of three general types. Luxuriant hemlock forests, now being decimated by the hemlock woolly adelgid (an Asian import), grow from 3,000 to 4,000 feet. Hardwoods grow from 4,000 feet to the summit spruce-fir zone. The damp, deep-soil valleys of the cove hardwood forests contain the park's tallest trees, often yellow poplar. Higher, above 4,500 feet, northern hardwoods of beech and birch intersperse among evergreens.

The Smokies' location and range of elevation bestows a uniquely northern climate. The best wildflower walks are invariably during April (with May a close second), as warm weather returns—especially lower in the park. Higher up, spring often hasn't sprung till very late May or early June. June, July, and August bring the warmest weather, but late August starts the temperature dip to autumn at lofty locations. By late September, autumn color is evident, and it's everywhere by mid- to late October.

Spring and summer are the Smokies' rainy season. There are beautiful days, but be prepared for misty rain, thunderstorms, and yes, even torrential downpours. Rainfall ranges between 55 and 85 inches annually, from low to high elevation—so rain gear should be in everyone's day pack. Fall generally dries out nicely—and quickly leads to winter.

The "Top of Old Smoky" is one long very high ridge that often influences the weather. From late October, and especially November through March and even into April, snow can be light and atmospheric (early and late) or drifted to awe-inspiring depths that close the Newfound Gap Road between Cherokee, North Carolina, and Gatlinburg, Tennessee. Spring and fall hikers should be prepared: Bring a hat, light gloves, and warm fleece garments to layer under waterproof outerwear should the wind whip and the temps dip. Winter hikers bound for the highest summits would do well to know the weather in advance and bring sophisticated winter gear and the expert knowledge of how to use it.

History

The Smokies are the perfect place to take a history hike. Evidence of times past is everywhere—especially along trails from late fall to spring, when retreating vegetation reveals walls, steps, foundations, and decaying structures.

Native American lore and legend wraps like the mists around these mountains, the once-idyllic realm of the Cherokee. Ironically, six years before Andrew Jackson banished the Smokies' Cherokees to their tragic Trail of Tears, a forced removal to Oklahoma in 1838, Hudson River School-era portrait artist George Catlin had proposed the concept of a "Nation's park" to protect "Indian civilization, wildlife, and wilderness" from destruction. Catlin's 1832 Indian portraits are among the classic images of the Old West. The proud Cherokee past stands out at various attractions just outside the park in the Cherokee Indians' Qualla Boundary reservation. The Oconaluftee River Trail near Cherokee is an introduction.

The arrival of later settlers is reflected in dozens of places, at sites where interpretive programs describe the lives of those whose early cabins, farms, mills, and later, clapboard churches and houses, still remain. In further irony, those residents were also evicted from the Smokies—but compensated for their property—when the National Park Service broadened the nation's environmental and recreational assets by creating parks in the East. In Virginia's Shenandoah National Park, then the Great Smokies in North Carolina and Tennessee, and again along the Blue Ridge Parkway in North Carolina and Virginia, the federal government removed residents from private land. Earlier parks in the West were created on public land to begin with.

The Smokies is one of the nation's premier places to savor the iconic, early settler style of structure called the log cabin. To get the most out of the park, pick up the booklet *Log Cabins of the Smokies* when you stop at one of the park's visitor centers, or get one online at the Great Smoky Mountains Association (www.smokiesstore.org). Other booklets feature the park's gristmills and churches.

Citizen Support of the Smokies

The Great Smoky Mountains Association (www.smokies store.org) and the Friends of the Smokies (www.friendsof thesmokies.org) are quintessential examples of the great work being done all over the nation by citizen groups that are raising money to bolster the shrinking budgets of individual parks. Some of these park support groups have special license plate programs (the "Friends" offer plates in both North Carolina and Tennessee) that dedicate the "vanity" fee to park programs. As befits our most visited national park, the two groups listed above are largely responsible for the insightful and inspiring interpretive efforts found all over the Smokies, including the trail brochures found at many paths. Indeed, these groups are actually funding an entirely new Oconaluftee Visitor Center for the Smokies (expected to be finished by late 2010). In short, as the park celebrated its seventy-fifth anniversary in 2009, there's no doubt that it is one of the most effectively interpreted parks in the nation.

Please do your part. Besides dropping a buck in the slot to buy a 50-cent trail brochure, please contribute at the trailheads and at visitor center donation boxes you'll see in the park. You won't need to hike more than a handful of trails in this book to become an enthusiastic supporter of the Smokies.

Trail Regulations

Camping

Backcountry campers are required to have an overnight permit that stipulates where and when they'll be camping—in essence, it's a reservation system. Permits can be obtained twenty-four hours a day by self-registering at many locations, including ranger stations, campground offices, and the Oconaluftee and Sugarlands visitor centers. Be aware that spaces at some popular shelter and campsites are rationed. If you intend to camp at one of those sites, you must phone in your registration to be sure there is space. Failure to do so is a ticketable offense. Your best bet is to call the Backcountry Reservation Office (open 8 a.m. to 6 p.m.; 865-436-1231) a month in advance of your first planned day on the trail.

Backcountry group size is limited to eight, and permits allow only one night of camping at a shelter and three nights at a backcountry campsite. Every Appalachian Trail shelter has a small number of spaces reserved for through-hikers, and short-distance backpackers get the rest. Campers must stay in designated sites and follow their itinerary. Do not reserve more space than needed and call to cancel if your plans change; failure to do so excludes other campers. Besides possessing your backcountry permit, you must camp and build fires only in designated sites. No tents are permitted at shelter sites (except by through-hikers who have no choice; call the Backcountry Information Office to clarify this and other regulations; open 9 a.m. to noon, 865-436-1297).

The Smokies are also home to the highest overnight accommodation in eastern America—LeConte Lodge, located atop Mount LeConte at 6,500 feet. Hiking to this full-service hostel is a ritual for many, and an experience akin to spending the night in one of the lofty hostels found in the European Alps. For more on this option, see the hike description for the Alum Cave Trail (the "easy way" to Mount LeConte).

Dogs

Dogs are permitted in campgrounds but must be leashed or enclosed at all times. They are prohibited on all trails, except a few, one of which is featured in this book (the Oconaluftee River Trail).

Safety and Precautions

Animals

For fans of wildlife, the Smokies are a bonanza of observational opportunities. Deer, black bears, and other animals are seen often, and wolves and elk are being reintroduced (the latter often glimpsed near roads along the Newfound Gap Road and in Cataloochee Valley). The more rarely glimpsed wild hogs were introduced from Europe into North Carolina as game in the early twentieth century and still remain. Hikers who take less traveled trails and tread softly will encounter many wild park residents. That said, taking some precautions will keep your encounters on the safe side.

Be Bear Aware

If you encounter a bear and attract its attention, the park's safety brochure says you are too close. Back away slowly and attempt to get as far away as possible. If a bear becomes aggressive and follows you, do not run and move off in a completely different direction. If the bear continues to approach, stand your ground, shout loudly, and act aggressively to scare the bear—even throw sticks and stones to run it off. You'll be more effective if you do this with a group of other hikers. If you are literally attacked, jettison your food and back out of the area. If you are being attacked and food is not the bear's objective, fight back in any way possible and with anything at hand.

In the backcountry, when not being carried or consumed, all food must be hung at least 10 feet off the ground to avoid tempting bears. All human feces must be buried at least 6 inches, and all toilet use must take place at least 100 feet from campsites and water sources.

Snakes

The Smokies' venomous vipers include the timber rattler and the copperhead, both mostly at mid- to lower elevations. Luckily, of the twenty-thousand people a year who are bitten by poisonous snakes in the United States, only between six and fifteen die. The low death rate is due to several factors: snake venom is relatively slow acting; almost half of all snakebites do not include the injection of venom; and antivenin is widely available at hospitals.

The park's venomous snakes are generally heftier than harmless snakes, and have triangular or arrow-shaped heads and vertically slit pupils (versus tube-shaped heads and round pupils for nonpoisonous snakes). To avoid snakes, don't reach blindly behind logs and rocks, inspect wooded sites where you plan to sit, and watch where you step.

When to Go

Any hike in the park can be crowded if you go at the wrong time, so choose carefully. Best bets: Visit the park and hike lower-elevation trails during late fall, early winter, or early spring. In spring, summer, or fall, try to hike midweek or go as early in the morning as possible. A crowded parking lot will not affect you if you return to one after your hike!

In spring or fall, choose the time just before or after wildflowers bloom or foliage peaks—and go midweek! And beyond encountering fewer people, consider visiting in winter, late fall, and early spring for the fact that the arrival of high-pressure weather systems brings increased visibility to the colder seasons. Ozone and other air pollutants have robbed the Smokies of its longest views, especially in summer. Winter and its shoulder months are much less affected—and that also bestows health benefits on anyone trying to hike in a national park that issues air pollution alerts when the adverse conditions might affect kids or anyone with breathing difficulties.

Bottom line: There's not much sense complaining about the crowds in the nation's most visited national park, especially if you come at a busy time. The Smokies are worth some vacation days. You will see fewer other folks if you choose less-visited seasons and visit midweek.

Sampling the Smokies

Motoring

This guide includes trails all over the Smokies, so don't assume that the popular and at times crowded Newfound Gap Road trailheads are your only entrances to the park. Both sides of the Smokies offer adventurous motor tours that abut nice trails.

The Cataloochee Valley, on the southeast side of the park, leads to great streamside strolls past the preserved churches, homes, and schools of early settlers. The appeal here includes possible sightings of the elk that are being reintroduced. In the south, the Heintooga Spur Road branches from the Blue Ridge Parkway near Maggie Valley and passes the parkway's Balsam Mountain Campground and Picnic Area to form a loop that reaches the Oconaluftee Visitor Center via the Cherokee reservation's Big Cove Road.

From Gatlinburg, don't miss the Roaring Fork Motor Nature Trail. Buy the brochure at the trailhead, take the hikes along the route that are listed in this book, and enjoy the historic and scenic sites of one of the park's best motor tours. Also from Gatlinburg and the Sugarlands Visitor Center, the Little River and Laurel Creek Roads lead to Elkmont Campground and the park's Cades Cove area—the latter featuring a truly spectacular and very popular 11-mile, one-way loop.

You'll also find access to these roads and Cades Cove from Townsend, Tennessee. Also near Townsend, the Rich Mountain Road and Parson Branch Road, both closed in winter, permit a visit to Cades Cove and exit via more lightly traveled roads through the heart of the park. Either or both of these roads are part of a big loop through and around the entire northwestern Smokies, using a portion of the Foothills Parkway (which is scheduled for extension).

Shuttle Services

Hiker shuttles are available from many companies just outside the park, so it's easy to start on one trail, hike out on another, and get a lift back to your car. Also keep in mind the Cherokee Transit option. The municipal transit authorities of Cherokee, Gatlinburg, and Pigeon Forge jointly operate comfortable buses that traverse the Newfound Gap Road many times a day (May through October), permitting hikers staying in any of these locations to get dropped off at a road-side trailhead and be picked up later for the ride back to their car (the Oconaluftee River Trail is one such option). Also, for older motorists, RV owners, or others who don't feel up to the drive across Newfound Gap, the shuttle service makes a ten-minute scenic stop at the gap and permits visitors to spend the day shopping or exploring a town on the other side of the Smokies—without having to use their own vehicle.

Surrounding Towns

The above road trips and shuttle options permit you to sample some of the Smokies' fascinating surrounding towns.

Cherokee

More than just another tourist town, Cherokee sits in the largest Indian reservation in eastern America. It is one of the premier destinations for parkway and Great Smokies visitors.

The Eastern Band of the Cherokee's stirring culture and history come alive in *Unto These Hills,* an outdoor drama that movingly tells the Trail of Tears saga (presented from early June to late August). The Museum of the Cherokee Indian has top-notch interactive exhibits. Oconaluftee Indian Village recreates a Cherokee town with rich hands-on demonstrations. Crafts and fine arts created by members of the oldest Native American art organization are available at the Qualla Arts and Crafts Mutual, Inc. (www.cherokee-nc.com). Granted, you'll see ticky-tacky tourist traps and souvenir stands, but the town has a beautiful river park and is undertaking successful efforts to upscale its appearance.

The reservation is also home to Harrah's Cherokee, a major casino with diverse dining, upscale decor, and a new golf course. You must be over twenty-one to enter the casino and a recent referendum made it the only place in Cherokee where beer and wine are available anywhere on the reservation. The Web site is www.harrahscherokee.com.

Nearby attractions include the Great Smoky Mountains Railroad in Bryson City (twenty minutes from Cherokee). Train excursions pass through Nantahala Gorge (one permits guests to raft their way back to town). The phone number is (800) 872-4681; the Web site is www.gsmr.com.

Also nearby is Nantahala Adventure Resort, or Nantahala Outdoor Center (NOC), which offers highly recommended rafting expeditions, an outfitter store, eateries, accommodations, and a great dose of southern Appalachian outdoor culture. Contact the NOC at 13077 Hwy. 19 West, Bryson City, NC 28713; (888) 905-7238; www.noc.com.

Gatlinburg/Pigeon Forge

These are the towns that Southerners think of when they conjure the term "touristy." Gatlinburg's major attractions run the gamut from wax museums to Ripley's Believe It or Not (www.gatlinburg.com). This is an attractive, pedestrian-friendly village that—were it not for the aforementioned tourist attractions—would remind some of a European mountain village, where creeks and rivers rush through town in rock-wall enclosed gushers and condos cluster around the village core.

This is a ski town from December to March, so the European feel is furthered by the huge aerial tram you can take from town up to the slopes for summertime ice skating and to see the town's black bear and eagle habitats. Gatlinburg has the park's most diverse dining and watering holes (with liquor and Alcoholic Beverage Control Commission/ABC stores available). There are all kinds of chain hotels and cabins tucked into the woods, including some of the park's historic sites, which are reached through Gatlinburg on the Cherokee Orchard Road and Roaring Fork Motor Nature Trail.

Pigeon Forge is a glitzy strip of popular family attractions with comedy, music, and Christian religious shows as the main draws (www.pigeonforgechamber.com or www.mypigeonforge.com). There are fun, high-quality museums devoted to Elvis and dinosaurs, and there's even a Titanic replica "docked" to the strip. Dolly Parton's "Dollywood"—simply one of the best theme parks in the nation—leads the list of attractions at Pigeon Forge (www.dollywood.com). The fare runs to down-home and wholesome—chow down on a country-style fried chicken dinner at Miss Lillian's Chicken House (named for Dolly's mother). The entertainment leans to pop and show tunes, but country, gospel, and mountain music are all appropriate to this southern Appalachian location, which gave us America's traditional music. You can watch the park's eagles and other birds of prey in a 30,000-square-foot aviary. And there's always the roller coasters—among the best in the country. Mystery Mine is a great ride, an adventure through an abandoned mine that kicks off with a 95-degree, 85-foot plunge into darkness. Thunderhead is the park's top thrill ride, a wooden roller coaster that drops riders 100 feet and hits a top speed of fifty-five miles per hour. The track even sends riders flying back through the loading station in mid-ride, giving waiting visitors a sneak peek at what's in store. The pool and health club at the modern new Pigeon Forge Community Center are also open to the public.

But of course—all this glitz is only icing on the real cake—Great Smoky Mountains National Park.

Zero Impact

Trails in the Great Smoky Mountains are heavily used year-round. We, as trail users and advocates, must be especially vigilant to make sure our passage leaves no lasting mark. Here are some basic guidelines for preserving trails:

- Pack out all your own trash, including biodegradable items like orange peels. You might also pack out garbage left by less considerate hikers.

- Don't approach or feed any wild creatures—the red squirrel eyeing your snack food is best able to survive if it remains self-reliant.

- Don't pick wildflowers or gather rocks, antlers, feathers, and other treasures along the trail. Removing these items will take away from the next hiker's experience.

- Avoid damaging trailside soils and plants by remaining on the established route. This is also a good rule of thumb for avoiding poison oak, ivy, sumac, and stinging nettle, common regional trailside irritants.

- Don't cut switchbacks, which can promote erosion.

- Be courteous by not making loud noises while hiking or at viewpoints, picnic spots, or campsites.

- Many Smokies trails are multiuse, which means you'll share them with other hikers, equestrians, trail runners, and in a few places, mountain bikers. Familiarize yourself with the proper trail etiquette, yielding the trail when appropriate.

- Use outhouses at trailheads or along the trail.

How to Use This Guide

This guide is designed to be simple and easy to use. Each hike is described with a map and summary information that delivers the trail's vital statistics including length, difficulty, fees and permits, park hours, canine compatibility, trail contacts, and best hiking season. Directions to the trailhead are also provided, along with a general description of what you'll see along the way. A detailed route finder (Miles and Directions) sets forth mileages between significant land-marks along the trail.

This book divides up the park into compass-direction quadrants. The Smokies' main ridge, basically the state line between Tennessee and North Carolina, roughly separates the park into northern and southern sections. The New-found Gap Road, US 441 between Cherokee and Gatlin-burg, cleaves the Smokies into eastern and western halves. Trails are thus featured in sections covering the northeast, southeast, southwest, and northwest parts of the park.

Difficulty Ratings

These are all easy hikes, but easy is a relative term. Some would argue that no hike involving a climb is easy, but the Smokies are among the East's highest mountains, so heading uphill and down are facts of life. To aid in the selection of a hike that suits particular needs and abilities, each is rated easy, moderate, or more challenging. Bear in mind that even most challenging routes can be made easy by hiking within your limits (turning around when you've had enough) and taking rests when you need them.

- **Easy** hikes are generally short and flat, taking no longer than an hour to complete.
- **Moderate** hikes involve increased distance and relatively mild changes in elevation, and will take one to two hours to complete.
- **More challenging** hikes feature some steep stretches, greater distances, and generally take longer than two hours to complete.

These are completely subjective ratings—consider that what you think is easy is entirely dependent on your level of fitness, sureness of foot, and the adequacy of your gear (primarily shoes or boots for more rugged terrain). If you are hiking with a group, you should select a hike with a rating that's appropriate for the least fit and prepared in your party.

Approximate hiking times are based on the assumption that on flat ground, most walkers average two miles per hour. Adjust that rate by the steepness of the terrain and your level of fitness (subtract time if you're an aerobic animal and add time if you're hiking with kids), and you have a ballpark hiking duration. Be sure to add more time if you plan to picnic or take part in other activities like bird watching or photography.

Trail Finder

Best Hikes for Peak Baggers

Best Hikes for Great Views

Best Hikes for Nature Lovers

Map Legend

══8══	Interstate Highway
══19══	U.S. Highway
══34══	State Highway
	Local Road
= = = = = =	Unpaved Road
▬▬▬▬▬▬	Featured Trail
- - - - - - - -	Trail
▬▬▬▬▬	Paved Trail
—··—··—	State Line
~~	River/Creek
⬚	National Park
⬚	Indian Reservation
🎭	Amphitheater
⛺	Camping
⍿	Gate
?	Information Center
🛏	Inn/Lodging
⌂	Observation Tower
P	Parking
▲	Peak
🅰	Picnic Area
■	Point of Interest/Structure
🍴	Restaurant
🚻	Restroom
~○	Spring
○	Town
⑪	Trailhead
🔭	Viewpoint/Overlook
≋	Waterfall

Northeast Section

1 Quiet Walkways

The Smokies' "Quiet Walkways" are great offerings—short strolls through sylvan settings along the Newfound Gap Road and in other places. They lead to very easy glimpses of nature and are often less busy than trails to specific points of interest. Some tie in to existing trails but most are segments of now-interrupted valley roads used by early settlers or loggers. These paths invite motorists to get out of their cars and stretch their legs. There are four along Newfound Gap Road between the Sugarlands Visitor Center and Newfound Gap.

Distance: Short out-and-back strolls; up to 0.5 mile.

Approximate hiking time: 30 minutes each, unless you dawdle

Difficulty: Easy

Trail surface: Usually flat and firm, sometimes grassy

Other trail users: None; no dogs or horses allowed

Best season: Year-round except when covered in snow or ice

Canine compatibility: Dogs not permitted

Fees and permits: None

Schedule: Closed only when inclement weather closes Newfound Gap Road

Trail contacts: Information about trails, camping, road closures, as well as downloadable maps and a "Smokies Trip Planner" are available online under the "Plan Your Visit" part of the park's excellent Web site, www.nps.gov/grsm. The Backcountry Information Office is open 9 a.m. to noon, 865-436-1297.

Finding the trailhead: Traveling south from Sugarlands Visitor Center, these paths are located on the left (east) at 1 mile, 1.7 miles, 2.3 miles, and 3.2 miles. Most are marked by small QUIET WALKWAY signs at the parking turnouts.

Kilometer

Mile

N

321

Gatlinburg

Foothill Parkway

441

Newfound Gap Road

Cherokee Orchard Road

Sugarlands Visitor
Information
Center

Little River Road

73

To Cades
Cove

1

2

West Prong Little Pigeon River

3

441

4

Sugarland
Mountain

To
Newfound
Gap

The Hike

The first Quiet Walkway (at 1 mile) explores a setting similar to the Sugarlands Nature Trail without the pavement or people. Bear right near the river to reach a nicely intact portion of the old valley road.

The walkway at 1.7 miles has handicapped parking and leads down a gradual old road grade to a bench where the Little Pigeon River is visible below (this is a favorite for fishing).

The walkway at 2.3 miles descends steeper switchbacks to the river and offers a rock-delineated section of the old road and evidence of early farming and settlement.

The walkway at 3.2 miles forms a little loop. Dip down the graveled path and go right above the river along a spectacular stone wall. At a gap in the wall, go left to the river and back to close the loop by hiking up past a bench.

2 Sugarlands Valley Self-Guiding Nature Trail

This fully accessible trail is a must–see Smokies experience for even the hard–core hiker. It is very well done, with wonderfully informative interpretive plaques as well as tactile exhibits for the visually impaired. This path conveys the appeal of the well–watered, verdant valleys that drew so many settlers to the foot of these high mountains.

Distance: 0.5-mile loop

Approximate hiking time: 30 to 45 minutes

Difficulty: Easy

Trail surface: Paved

Other trail users: None; no dogs or horses allowed

Best season: Early summer

Canine compatibility: Dogs not permitted

Fees and permits: None

Schedule: Closed only when inclement weather closes Newfound Gap Road

Maps: USGS Gatlinburg; TOPO! Tennessee, Kentucky

Trail contacts: Information about trails, camping, road closures, as well as downloadable maps and a "Smokies Trip Planner" are available online under the "Plan Your Visit" part of the park's excellent Web site, www .nps.gov/grsm. The Backcountry Information Office is open 9 a.m. to noon, 865-436-1297.

Special considerations: A nature trail brochure is available to buy at the trailhead.

Finding the trailhead: The trail starts on the east side of Newfound Gap Road, 0.4 mile south of Sugarlands Visitor Center and 13 miles north of Newfound Gap. GPS: N35 40.770' / W83 31.873'

The Hike

You'll be nicely acquainted with this and other Smokies lowland valley locations once you've traveled this trail. From the early 1800s, the rough road through Sugarlands Valley was the main route between Gatlinburg, or White Oak Flats, and the Cherokee area of North Carolina. Farms and communities spread up the lower sections and logging here was lighter than at many places in what is now the park. In the ninety or so years since farmers, loggers, and even the first trickle of vacation-home builders left the fledgling national park, there's been a dramatic reclamation by nature.

The loop splits just past a bridge with an embedded bench. There's no arrow, but go left (east). Two startling river-rock chimneys appear in the trail's first curves, all that remain of some of the Smokies' earliest vacation homes (circa 1900). Not far beyond, at brochure stop 3, a side shoot of the paved trail leads left (east), where the old road is particularly identifiable beside the West Prong Little Pigeon River as it rushes all along this side of the trail. This path's artfully weaving exploration of the terrain is itself an aesthetic experience. Keep your eyes peeled throughout this hike for evidence of other walls and rock piles—the trail passes right through one stout stone wall.

All along the trail, bas-relief plaques present opportunities for the visually impaired to touch the shapes of leaves, fish (more than sixty species are found in the park), salamanders (more here than in any other spot in North America), poison ivy, the deeply-grooved bark of sourwood, and more.

The trail turns along the end of the loop at 0.3 mile and kids can easily step off and down to a small side stream running

Sugarlands Valley Self-Guiding Nature Trail

0   Kilometer   0.25
0   Mile   0.25

N

To Gatlinburg

441

Twomile Branch

Park Headquarters

Twomile Lead

To Cades Cove

Sugarlands Visitor Information Center

Little River Road

73

West Prong Little Pigeon River

P
2

Sugarlands Valley Self-Guiding Nature Trail

Newfound Gap Road

beneath the Newfound Gap Road not far away. As the loop nears its junction, one insightful sign shows the stages of forest recovery after settlement with a depiction of the scene beside the trail that includes the cabins that once stood by the chimneys in the distance.

If you'd like to see other defined sections of the old road across the Smokies, consider a few of the nearby quiet walkways under Hike 1 or take the loftier Chimney Tops Trail. Where that trail turns right/west (at 0.9 mile), follow the Road Prong Trail left (south, then east) as far as you care to walk.

3 Noah "Bud" Ogle Self-Guiding Trail

This great hike is recommended for easy roadside access to historic structures and a longer super–scenic streamside stretch that'll make you feel like you've walked into an early photo of hardscrabble backwoods life in the Smokies.

Distance: 0.7-mile loop
Approximate hiking time: 1 hour or less
Difficulty: Easy
Trail surface: This trail is a snap if you just visit the buildings. But the longer loop of the path, though gradual, follows a rocky old road and crosses boulder gardens on a less-than-level stone pathway.
Other trail users: None
Best season: Spring or late fall/winter, to either sense the promise of a new Smokies' planting season (and great wildflowers), or to grasp the bleaker prospect of months to go in these mountains without fresh food
Canine compatibility: Dogs not permitted
Fees and permits: None
Schedule: Open year-round, except rarely after snowfall and before plowing
Maps: USGS Le Conte; TOPO!

Tennessee, Kentucky
Trail contacts: Information about trails, camping, road closures, as well as downloadable maps and a "Smokies Trip Planner" are available online under the "Plan Your Visit" part of the park's excellent Web site, www .nps.gov/grsm. The Backcountry Information Office is open 9 a.m. to noon, 865-436-1297.

Special considerations: Don't turn around on Cherokee Orchard Road to get back to Gatlinburg—continue around the 5-mile one-way Roaring Fork Motor Nature Trail, one of the park's best motor tours (open mid Mar to late Nov; no trailers, buses, or trucks allowed). A trailhead brochure is available and turnouts enable stops that highlight historic structures and spectacular scenery. You're also likely to glimpse wildlife, including bears. The Grotto Falls hike is also on this route.

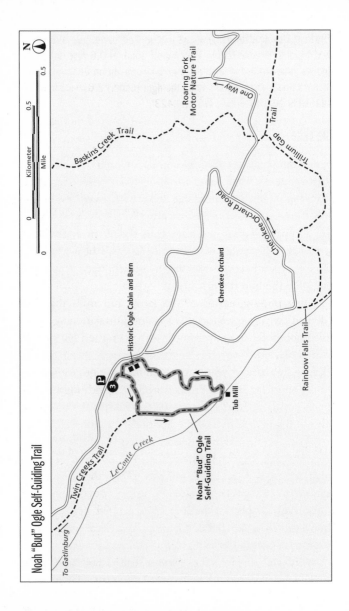

Noah "Bud" Ogle Self-Guiding Trail

To Gatlinburg

Twin Creeks Trail

LeConte Creek

Historic Ogle Cabin and Barn

P

3

Noah "Bud" Ogle
Self-Guiding Trail

Tub Mill

Cherokee Orchard

Cherokee Orchard Road

Baskins Creek Trail

Roaring Fork
Motor Nature Trail

One Way

Trillium Gap
Trail

Rainbow Falls Trail

N

Kilometer
0   0.5

Mile
0   0.5

Finding the trailhead: From US 441 in Gatlinburg, turn at traffic light #8 onto Historic Nature Trail/Airport Road. In 0.6 mile, keep right (southeast) at the junction, then stay straight on Cherokee Orchard Road. The trailhead is on the right (south) 2.6 miles from US 441. GPS: N35 41.008' / W83 29.423'

The Hike

Few visitors to the Smokies today would fail to agree that the decision to found the park was a wise one. Then again—no one alive now can look back over a shoulder at a former home in what is today America's most visited national park. You can only imagine the plight of displaced residents. This trail movingly conveys the beauty of the place they left behind—and the investment needed to carve out a life there in the first place.

Only photos remain of the farms and mills that had "defiled" what we see today as a major mountain range pristine enough for the government to have turned out people from a place they called home. One of them, Noah "Bud" Ogle, gazes back at you from the trailhead sign. Luckily, if you're short for time, a breeze through his beautiful hand-crafted cabin and barn is only 100 yards from the trailhead. An old road grade rises to the left of the buildings.

But to really savor this site, which means seeing the structures last, bear right (southwest) not far from the trailhead, before the log buildings, and follow the nature trail sign on an easy grade out into the woods. Beyond post #3 you'll cross a split log bridge, and bear left past post #5 on an old road that linked Gatlinburg to local farms along boulder-strewn LeConte Creek.

At a trail junction, the Twin Creeks Trail heads right (northwest), leading 1.8 miles to Gatlinburg (add an out-

and-back trek on this gradual path if you like). Beyond, the Bud Ogle trail dips down through a section of old road lined with rock walls past post #7 and a huge pile of rocks, remnants of a cabin used to let young couples have a home until their own could be completed. Just beyond, an unusual evergreen cluster of tall skinny boxwoods further marks the home site. Off in the woods to the far right there's extensive evidence of other walls.

The trail swings left (south) up the creek past a stunning old tub mill sitting in a stream. Step inside if you like. The log flumes convey water down to strike the metal wheel (at one time enclosed in a "tub" (hence the name), but later left open). The Ogles used it to grind their own and neighbors' grain.

When the trail rises across a lush fern- and moss-covered rib of rocks and boulders scattered through the woods, you'll wonder how anyone could have farmed this area. Cross a bridge made of a massive log and at post #11, it's a lot easier to imagine that this area was a field of crops before the forest grew up.

You'll return to the farm buildings from above as you cross a small stream by the barn. Glance inside, then wander down the old road to the right. The water here was funneled to the farm house via log flumes. Explore the cabin, expanded as years went by on both sides of the fireplace (which was never quite fully enclosed to avoid the risk of fire).

Miles and Directions

- **0.0** Begin at the trailhead on the south side of Cherokee Orchard Road.
- **0.2** Reach the stone wall section of the old road.
- **0.4** Arrive at the tub mill.
- **0.7** Arrive back at the trailhead.

4 Grotto Falls

Grotto Falls is a place where anyone can experience the cinema fantasy of standing behind a waterfall (though don't expect to be completely hidden back here). Grotto Falls shoots off a semicircular ledge, and the trail artfully swings behind and below the cascade.

Distance: 2.6 miles out and back

Approximate hiking time: 2 hours

Difficulty: Moderate

Trail surface: Packed soil with firm footing, but the clay sections can be slick after rain

Other trail users: Llama teams regularly use this trail (Mon, Wed, and Fri) to resupply Le Conte Lodge with food and necessities for guests, so you can arrange to see them padding along. They usually begin their trek by 8 a.m. and can often be seen returning from the lodge by 4 p.m. or so. To double-check the latest schedule, call (865) 429-5704.

Best season: Spring for flowers and stream flow. Also midweek; this is a popular trail

Canine compatibility: Dogs not permitted

Fees and permits: None

Schedule: mid-Mar to late Nov

Maps: USGS Mount Le Conte; TOPO! Tennessee, Kentucky

Trail contacts: Information about trails, camping, road closures, as well as downloadable maps and a "Smokies Trip Planner" are available online under the "Plan Your Visit" part of the park's excellent Web site, www .nps.gov/grsm. The Backcountry Information Office is open 9 a.m. to noon, 865-436-1297.

Special considerations: Grotto Falls is not far from Gatlinburg, and it's also on one of the busier trails to Mount Le Conte. If you want to avoid crowds, choose shoulder or off-seasons and arrive early to find parking space in the lot.

Other: Reaching Grotto Falls requires taking the 5-mile one-way Roaring Fork Motor Nature

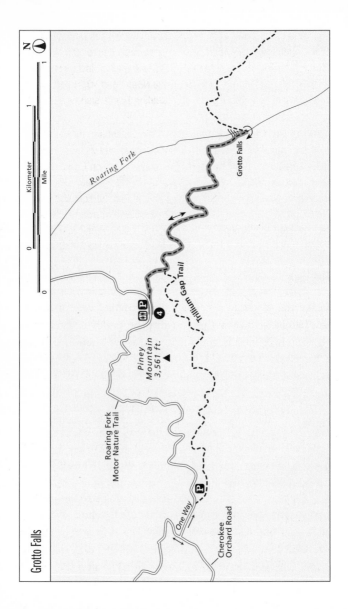

Grotto Falls

N

Kilometer
0   1

Mile
0   1

Roaring Fork

Grotto Falls

Trillium Gap Trail

Piney Mountain
3,561 ft.

Roaring Fork
Motor Nature Trail

One Way

Cherokee
Orchard Road

Trail, one of the park's best motor tours (open from mid-Mar to late Nov; no trailers, buses, or trucks allowed). A trailhead brochure is available and turnouts include historic structures and spectacular scenery. You're also likely to glimpse wildlife, including bears. The Noah "Bud" Ogle Self-Guiding Trail is also on this route.

Finding the trailhead: From US 441 in Gatlinburg, turn at traffic light #8 onto Historic Nature Trail/Airport Road. In 0.6 mile, keep right (southeast) at the junction, then stay straight on Cherokee Orchard Road. At 3.6 miles (1 mile past the Noah "Bud" Ogle nature trail parking area), turn right (east) onto the Roaring Fork Motor Nature Trail. The Trillium Gap Trail parking area for Grotto Falls is on the left (north) 5.2 miles from US 441 (1.7 miles from the motor nature trail entrance). GPS: N35 40 49.540' / W83 27.750'

The Hike

Leave the lot amid a verdant old-growth forest of towering hemlocks now suffering from the park's infestation of the hemlock woolly adelgid. One "wow" hemlock is just a short way up the trail. Go left (southeast) at the junction with the Trillium Gap Trail, 0.2 mile above the parking area. As the trail winds higher, it rises gradually through mature cove hardwood forest and delves into, then out of, the first stream crossing. That's a prominent feature of this trail—the way it weaves in and out around the dramatic leading ridges of Mount Le Conte, the park's single most massive summit.

The wet clay trail surface past the first stream—and in many spots on this route—can be slick when wet. The trail is so popular that roots across the path are worn flat. Nevertheless, choose an off-time and you can almost be alone. The grade grows much more gradual after the second stream crossing (one of five to the falls, if you're counting). The third easy stream hop presents a pretty little cascade in the crotch of the ridge, and at the fourth, the trees tower over a suddenly uniform understory of glossy green rhododendron. Out around the next ridge, the fifth stream drainage has the much deeper voice of a real cascade somewhere above. Soon you'll see a fine fall left of the trail with a deep pool and a log spanning it. Farther above you'll see another cataract. Yep, that's Grotto Falls.

The trail rises to boulders at the falls' base and just beyond the trail winds behind the showering water. If you can catch this trail at a really off-time, the sight of the falls cascading into the rocky defile, devoid of hikers in bright outdoor gear, will recall nineteenth-century lithographs of America's romantic wilderness. Photo tip: This is the place to know how to use your shutter delay button so you don't have to hand-hold your camera. Whether you put the camera on a tripod or find a rock to set it on, a very slow shutter speed will create that milky blur that makes for such good waterfall photos.

Miles and Directions

- **0.0** Start by venturing into the old-growth hemlock forest.
- **0.2** Reach the junction with the Trillium Gap Trail and go left (southeast).
- **1.3** Arrive at Grotto Falls (the turnaround point)
- **2.6** Arrive back at the trailhead.

5 Ramsay Cascades

Reaching one of the Smokies' highest and most scenic waterfalls requires a long but not too taxing day hike. The trip into this well-watered, rhododendron-rich watershed is made all the more special by one of the park's most impressive big forests.

Distance: 8 miles out and back
Approximate hiking time: 4 to 5 hours
Difficulty: More challenging
Trail surface: Starts on a old forest road then becomes a wooded trail with rocks, roots, muddy spots, and a rocky scramble at the end
Other trail users: None; no dogs or horses allowed
Best season: Best in spring for flowers, and for the falls after a rainy spell
Canine compatibility: Dogs not permitted
Fees and permits: None
Schedule: Significant winter snow could restrict access
Maps: USGS Mount Guyot; TOPO! Tennessee, Kentucky
Trail contacts: Information about trails, camping, road closures, as well as downloadable maps and a "Smokies Trip Planner" are available online under the "Plan Your Visit" part of the park's excellent Web site, www .nps.gov/grsm. The Backcountry Information Office is open 9 a.m. to noon, 865-436-1297.
Special considerations: The Smokies are notorious for fatalities at waterfalls. Do not be tempted to climb this or any Smokies cascade.

Finding the trailhead: Leave Gatlinburg with a turn from US 441 onto eastbound US 321 at stoplight #3. In 6 miles, turn right (south) into the national park on Greenbrier Road. The road goes gravel beyond the Greenbrier Ranger Station where, at 3 miles, you turn left (east) at the fork. Continue for another 1.5 miles to the trailhead. GPS: N35 42 10.290' / W83 21.417'

Ramsay Cascades

Ramsay Prong Road

Greenbrier Pinnacle
4,997 ft.

Discontinued Trail to
Greenbrier Pinnacle

Devils Den
3,375 ft.

Ramsay Cascades Trail

Ramsay Prong

Middle Prong Little Pigeon River

Ramsay Cascades

Bald Top Ridge
3,425 ft.

Kilometer

Mile

N

The Hike

Ramsay Cascades must have an identity crisis. Over the years it's been consistently spelled inconsistently, with either "sey" or a "say" at the end. Southern Appalachian family names had a way of evolving over time—this is another example.

The 1.5 miles, on a very gradual forest road, makes a nice stroll without going all the way to the waterfall. The long bridge not far from the trailhead is another of those great Smokies opportunities to snag a photo from the middle of a rushing, wild stream amidst lush rhododendron (the Boogerman Trail offers another such opportunity, also not far from the road).

Past the end of the dirt road, the route explores increasingly deep woods as the trail follows the Middle Prong of the Little Pigeon River. You'll cross a bridge at just more than 2 miles, then follow Ramsay Prong through dense, rich rhododendron forests that rise left (north) up to Greenbrier Pinnacle and right (south) up to Guyot Spur. This route though impressively towering trees delves deep into a cleft that runs all the way up to the Smokies' crest and Mount Guyot (6,621 feet), the fourth highest peak in eastern America—second highest in the park and the highest mountain in the East that does not have a formal trail to its summit.

At 3 miles, cross a bridge to the left (north) bank of Ramsay Prong, and for the next 0.7 mile walk through an inspiring cove hardwood forest in an area that escaped the logger's saw. Big poplars dominate the forest. The final few tenths of a mile to the waterfall is steep, rocky, and wet, so prepare to take it easy and watch your footing. This waterfall is worth the effort.

Miles and Directions

0.0   Start on a gradual forest road.

1.5   Leave the dirt road on a woodsy trail.

3.0   Cross the last big bridge to the north side of Ramsay Prong.

4.0   Reach Ramsay Cascades.

8.0   Arrive back at the trailhead.

6 Appalachian Trail to the Jumpoff and Charlies Bunion

A walk on the storied Georgia-to-Maine footpath rises from Newfound Gap to fabulous views at the Jumpoff and the craggy perch of Charlies Bunion.

Distance: 6.5 miles out and back to the Jumpoff; 8 miles out and back to Charlies Bunion

Approximate hiking time: 7 hours

Difficulty: More challenging due to elevation gain, but the hike requires stamina and a sense of adventure due to the distance and rocky character of the Appalachian Trail

Trail surface: The slope is relatively gradual but the trail is rocky and eroded in places

Other trail users: None; no dogs or horses allowed

Best season: Winter, late fall, and early spring, as much for the lack of other hikers as for the fact that the arrival of high pressure weather systems bring increased visibility to the colder seasons

Canine compatibility: Dogs not permitted

Fees and permits: None

Schedule: Unavailable only when inclement weather closes Newfound Gap Road

Maps: USGS Mount Le Conte and Mount Guyot; TOPO! Tennessee, Kentucky; TOPO! North Carolina, South Carolina

Trail contacts: Information about trails, camping, road closures, as well as downloadable maps and a "Smokies Trip Planner" are available online under the "Plan Your Visit" part of the park's excellent Web site, www.nps.gov/grsm. The Backcountry Information Office is open 9 a.m. to noon, 865-436-1297.

Special considerations: Be prepared to see a lot of other hikers. Aim for an early start on an off-season weekday.

Other: This is one of only a few hikes in this book that is not easy. But the hike is included

Appalachian Trail to the Jumpoff and Charlies Bunion

N

Kilometer
0   1

Mile
0   1

Charlies Bunion

The Jumpoff

Icewater Spring Shelter

Appalachian Trail

The Boulevard Trail

To Mount LeConte

Kephart Prong Trail

Sweat Heifer Creek

Sweat Heifer Creek Trail

441

Newfound Gap Road

To Gatlinburg

6

P

To Cherokee

because it is among the easiest high-adventure hikes often hiked by well-equipped, motivated novices in good shape.

Finding the trailhead: The major trailhead parking area is on Newfound Gap Road, 13 miles from Sugarlands Visitor Center south of Gatlinburg in Tennessee, and 16 miles from Oconaluftee Visitor Center north of Cherokee, North Carolina. Leave the north side of the parking lot just beyond the trail to the restrooms. GPS: N35 36.663' / W83 25.493'

The Hike

Newfound Gap may be a truly popular place to start a hike, but this trailhead is also the best way to reach a few of the Smokies' most spectacular viewpoints. From the memorial to the Rockefeller Foundation, whose funds helped found the park (President Franklin Delano Roosevelt dedicated the park here in 1940), day hikes reach two awesome views: the Jumpoff and Charlies Bunion.

Leaving the gap, the trail was one of the first built-from-scratch sections of the Appalachian Trail (AT), artfully excavated by the Civilian Conservation Corps (CCC). Though gradual, it's now badly eroded, rocky, and rooty in places as it rises from gap to gap, past the Sweat Heifer Creek Trail on the right (southeast) at 1.7 miles, to reach The Boulevard Trail on the left (northwest) at 2.7 miles. The Boulevard is a sharp evergreen ridge that leads 5.4 miles to the summit of Mount LeConte (6,593 feet), home to LeConte Lodge, open from late March into November, and the Mount LeConte shelter.

To reach the Jumpoff (6,100 feet), go left (northwest) on The Boulevard Trail a short distance and turn right (north) at the trail sign, heading up the rocky start. The trail crosses

6,150-foot Mount Kephart to a cliff-top view that looks down more than 1,000 feet and out ahead (east) to Charlies Bunion. The round-trip hike to the Jumpoff and back to Newfound Gap is 6.5 miles.

One of the most scenic sections of trail in the Smokies leads from the Jumpoff trail junction to Charlies Bunion. Continuing north on the AT (left if you turn from The Boulevard Trail), the trail to Icewater Spring Shelter appears on the right (east) in 0.3 mile. At 3.8 miles (from Newfound Gap), the two rocky peaks that make up Charlies Bunion testify to the devastation that logging, forest fires, and sub-sequent floods caused before the park existed. All three denuded this area before 1930, and today the sparse vegetation makes the crags appear almost alpine. Go left on the short loop that circles this truly spectacular—but lamentably named—beauty spot. The round-trip hike is about 8 miles.

Miles and Directions

0.0 Start from Newfound Gap on the Appalachian Trail.

1.7 Pass the Sweat Heifer Creek Trail on the right (southeast).

2.7 Reach the junction with The Boulevard Trail. Go left (northwest) here, then right (north) for the Jumpoff. It is 1 mile out and back from this intersection to the viewpoint and 6.5 miles round-trip from the Newfound Gap trailhead.

3.0 The path to Icewater Spring Shelter goes right (east).

3.9 Head left (north) to circle Charlies Bunion.

8.0 Arrive back at the trailhead.

7 Alum Cave Trail to Mount LeConte

Mount LeConte is the park's most spectacular summit, and the cozy cabins and cottages of LeConte Lodge, not to mention bountiful (but simple) meals, make an overnight on this peak one of eastern America's real adventures. It's not easy, but because there's food and a warm bed waiting on top (for those who can get a reservation!), this memorable hike is often tackled by well-equipped, motivated novices in good shape. It'd be a lot more difficult if you were backpacking!

Distance: 10 miles out and back

Approximate hiking time: 4 to 5 hours up, 2 to 3 hours down

Difficulty: More challenging

Trail surface: Rocky, steep forest trail that can have ice and snow in spots in spring and fall, and deep drifts in winter

Other trail users: None

Best season: Whenever you can get a reservation—but be sure to avoid very early and late in the year unless you love and can handle cold, snow, and ice.

Canine compatibility: Dogs not permitted

Fees and permits: None for hiking; fee for lodge accommodations.

Schedule: Unavailable only when inclement weather closes Newfound Gap Road. LeConte Lodge

open from late March to late November.

Maps: USGS Mount LeConte; TOPO! Tennessee, Kentucky

Trail contacts: Information about trails, camping, road closures, as well as downloadable maps and a "Smokies Trip Planner" are available online under the "Plan Your Visit" part of the park's excellent Web site, www .nps.gov/grsm. The Backcountry Information Office is open 9 a.m. to noon, 865-436-1297. LeConte Lodge; (865) 429-5704; www.leconte-lodge.com; reservations@leconte-lodge.com

Special considerations: This is one of only a few hikes in this book that is not easy, but was selected because the route is the easiest way to tackle a high-

adventure hike. Do not undertake this trek lightly, but know that it is often hiked by well-prepared hikers in good shape.
Other: Special weather warning—expect potentially severe weather. You'll sleep in a propane-heated cabin, but flatlanders should bring layered, weatherproof garments (a hat and gloves included).

Finding the trailhead: The big Alum Cave parking areas lie on the east side of Newfound Gap Road 8.8 miles south from the Sugarlands Visitor Center, and 4.4 miles north of Newfound Gap. Adding The Boulevard Trail option requires spotting a car at Newfound Gap (where restrooms are available). GPS: N35 37.730' / W83 27.051'

The Hike

The trek to Tennessee's LeConte Lodge is the Great Smokies' only true "hut hike," like those in the White Mountains of New Hampshire and the Alps of Europe, where you carry a light pack and find meals and overnight accommodations in a high mountain hostel. It's great fun.

Mount LeConte and its lodge are a premier experience, so much so that many, many regulars come back year after year to test their fitness against the march of time—and exercise their "grandfathered" right to ongoing reservations. Starting in 1987, hikers from the prior year have been given first dibs on the same date the next year. Many have done so, seemingly for decades since. For that reason, reservations are hard to get for the "general public," but worth the effort. Your best bet is to e-mail (or fax/mail) the reservation form before "reservations open for the year," generally in early October for the following year (the hut operates from late March to just before Thanksgiving). Calling after the reservation "opening" date is also an option. Just hit "redial" and devote some time to getting through. If you want to get in, you may need to take any date that is available. If no reservations are available, ask to get on the waiting list. The closer you are to first on the list, the more likely you are to get in, so call early in the day. The list is maintained in ten-day time frames, so if you don't make the cut, you need to re-reserve for the next ten days.

Hikers who get a reservation and use this style of back-country lodging carry relatively light packs, with clothing, toiletries, and snacks, and the "hut" provides a bed and meals. Guests at LeConte stay in cabins, some of which can accommodate one or a few families. There are flush toilets (no showers) and a dining building, where guests enjoy hearty meals that can include wine, and a separate relaxation lodge with board games and more.

Head out on one of the Smokies' most memorable hikes by crossing the first of many impressive log bridges that will carry you across the streams that enliven the lower half of this trail. Past the second bridge across Alum Cave Creek, the gradual, steadily rising Alum Cave Trail turns left (north) into the Styx Branch drainage and then swings out to Arch Rock at 1.4 miles. Crossing a bridge below the cleft, the trail turns left (southwest) and climbs a steep flight of curving steps through a large arch of eroded rock. Leaving Styx Branch, the trail reaches the apex of the ridge and great views at Inspiration Point. Not far beyond, the massive overhang of Alum Cave Bluffs towers overhead at 2.3 miles. It's a short but steep and impressive climb along and under its sheltering brow. Turn around here for a 4.6-mile hike to one of the park's scenic high points. A worthwhile interpretive brochure to this lower part of the trail is available at the sign near the trailhead parking lot.

From the bluffs on, LeConte rears up and the trail becomes a ridge walk suitable to a major summit. Views open above to the mountain's four peaks. Some of the most exciting terrain arrives as you slab left (west) from the ridge to carve across the high flank of the summit, at times through grassy landslides and across ledges with cables strung along the rock for safety. You'll sigh as the trail levels through spruce and fir, passes the junction with the Rainbow Falls Trail on the left (north), and reveals the lodge's collection of cabins to the left (northeast).

Nearby viewpoints beckon. Cliff Top is the closest to the lodge, and looks west to the sunset. Where the steps descend left to the lodge, the trail to Cliff Top goes right (west). It reaches a great view, where sedge grasses grow down the cliff face to the right, and the parking area of Newfound Gap is far off to the left (southwest). The trail then loops left (east) and joins The Boulevard Trail beyond the lodge. Myrtle Point, farther beyond—in fact, past the mountain's summit—looks east toward the sunrise. Both are ritual excursions for lodge guests. Looking west may be best.

The elevation drop from LeConte to Gatlinburg is impressive—it's a very direct vertical mile from the summit. That kind of relief is found in the Rockies more often than the Appalachians—and a variety of publications say that makes LeConte the tallest mountain in the park, or the East, when measured from base to summit.

Option
If your party has two cars you can start or end a 13.1-mile summit loop at Newfound Gap by walking the 5.4-mile evergreen knife-edge ridge of The Boulevard Trail, one

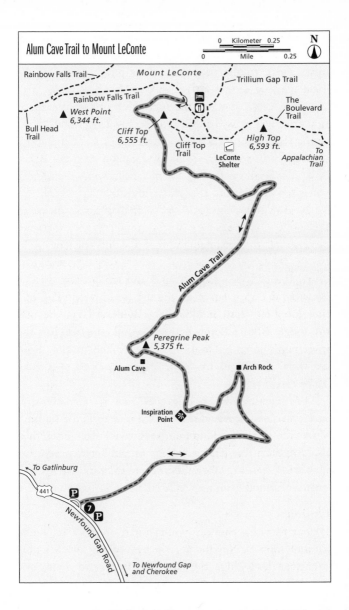

Alum Cave Trail to Mount LeConte

0 — Kilometer — 0.25
0 — Mile — 0.25

N

Rainbow Falls Trail

Mount LeConte

Trillium Gap Trail

Rainbow Falls Trail

The Boulevard Trail

Bull Head Trail

▲ West Point 6,344 ft.

▲

Cliff Top 6,555 ft.

Cliff Top Trail

LeConte Shelter

High Top 6,593 ft. ▲

To Appalachian Trail

Alum Cave Trail

↕

Peregrine Peak 5,375 ft. ▲

■ Arch Rock

■ Alum Cave

Inspiration Point

↔

To Gatlinburg

441

P

7

P

Newfound Gap Road

To Newfound Gap and Cherokee

of the most spectacular experiences in the park. Starting from Newfound Gap (at 5,048 feet, versus 3,800 feet at the Alum Cave Trail parking area), this is a longer route to the hut, involves less of a climb, and is probably less strenuous (despite the last climb to the LeConte summit). You could also leave LeConte and descend The Boulevard Trail to the AT (at 2.7 miles from Newfound Gap); turn right (southwest) on the AT, and continue to Newfound Gap for an 8.1-mile exit. The significant drawbacks in that direction are that The Boulevard Trail ends with a cruelly steep climb to the Appalachian Trail. And the AT, though not steep on the way down to Newfound Gap, is eroded, rocky, and not an easy walk. Nevertheless, The Boulevard Trail is one of the park's high points. It crosses an amazing landslide, with a cable to hang onto, not far below LeConte's peak. This wonderfully designed and well-maintained trail is almost always on the crest of a memorably sharp ridge.

Truth is, the hike up and down Alum Cave Trail is the easiest way to see LeConte.

Miles and Directions

0.0 Start by heading east from the parking lot on the Alum Cave Trail.

1.4 Reach Arch Rock.

2.3 Arrive at Alum Cave Bluffs, a potential turnaround spot.

5.0 Reach the summit of Mount LeConte.

10.0 Arrive back at the trailhead.

8 Cosby Self-Guiding Nature Trail

This trail is much more than a campground leg–stretcher. The designer of this trail must have been an artist. The way the trail offers up the virgin forest experience is almost as impressive as the setting itself.

Distance: 1-mile loop

Approximate hiking time: 1 hour plus

Difficulty: Easy

Trail surface: Packed soil or gravel with some rocky sections and old asphalt

Other trail users: None; no dogs or horses allowed

Best season: Year-round

Canine compatibility: Dogs not permitted

Fees and permits: None

Schedule: Significant winter snow could restrict access.

Maps: USGS Hartford; TOPO! Tennessee, Kentucky

Trail contacts: Information about trails, camping, road closures, as well as downloadable maps and a "Smokies Trip Planner" are available online under the "Plan Your Visit" part of the park's excellent Web site, www .nps.gov/grsm. The Backcountry Information Office is open 9 a.m. to noon, 865-436-1297.

Special considerations: This trail is so nice that you might consider camping at Cosby Campground just to take this hike. Further, consider that a vastly improved Cosby Campground reopened in spring 2010, making it one of the best maintained campgrounds in the park. Stimulus funding repaved the campground for the first time since the 1960s and made other facility improvements possible.

Finding the trailhead: From the US 321/TN 32 junction, about 15.4 miles east of Gatlinburg, turn right (southeast) and drive 1.2 miles. Turn right (south) again on the signed Cosby Campground road. Drive 2 miles and take the first left into the picnic area as you approach the campground. Swing along past the picnic sites (where restrooms and water are available seasonally) and up to the right into the hikers' parking area, just below the campground entrance kiosk. GPS: N35 45.361' / W83 12.475'

The Hike

This amble not far from the drainage of Crying Creek is so scenic it could almost bring tears to your eyes. Drop past the mileage sign to an atmospheric old road grade and go right (south) on the Low Gap Trail, following the NATURE TRAIL sign. Fine views look down onto the rushing stream in a mature cove hardwood forest. Pass the side trail on the right to the amphitheater parking area (actually the "formal" start of the nature trail, where the trail brochure is available at a trailhead dispenser). Continue below the nicely refurbished amphitheater to cross a ford on the old road at the trail's first numbered post.

Go left (east) past the ford to cross two log bridges and wander down between streams in a tall forest alive with water. This is the inspiring grove you were earlier looking down upon—a richly tangled virgin forest lush with ferns and moss. Also notice the extensive growths of partridge-berry that thrives along this trail. The plant (with many medicinal uses for Native Americans) flowers in early spring (with twin blossoms) and enlivens a winter hike with mats of small evergreen leaves and red autumn berries that feed wildlife throughout the cold season.

As you wander down and to the right among wet and dry drainages, old remnants of asphalt paving crop up. On the left, past post #4, sits a startlingly intertwined maple and birch—both germinated atop a fallen log that long ago decayed, leaving them standing on stiltlike roots. More streams appear to the right (east) and the trail crosses two

Cosby Self-Guiding Nature Trail

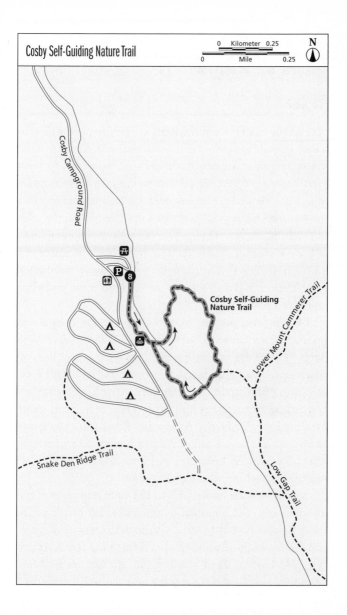

more bridges. Turning uphill, there's a trailside view of a little pool and cascade. Wandering higher between streams, amid a truly impressive cathedral of trees, the trail crosses another log bridge. There's no numbered post here, but if there were one it'd be labeled "Fallen Giant" in the trail brochure. A mammoth uprooted hardwood lies directly across the trail, nicely sawed to permit passage. The rushing stream pouring past its shallow roots—and high wind or ice?—spelled this tree's demise. At post #8, a rock-wall enclosure sits to the left and a fallen chimney scatters to the right. Beyond, the trail follows a moss-covered stone wall that also leads to a stream on the right. Imagine living in such a place.

At a T junction with the Low Gap Trail, go right (west), across two log bridges to the old road grade you started on. Turn right, descending past the amphitheater to the trailhead.

Miles and Directions

0.0 Start on the old road grade.

0.2 Turn left (northeast) from the old road onto the nature trail.

0.7 Turn right (southwest) at the junction with the Low Gap Trail.

1.0 Arrive back at the trailhead.

Southeast Section

9 Quiet Walkways

The Smokies' Quiet Walkways are great offerings—short strolls through sylvan settings along the Newfound Gap Road and other locations. They lead to very easy glimpses of nature and are often less busy than trails to specific points of interest. Some tie in to existing trails but most are segments of now interrupted old roads used by settlers or loggers. These paths invite motorists to stretch their legs and return. There are five along Newfound Gap Road between the Oconaluftee Visitor Center and Newfound Gap.

Distance: Short out-and-back strolls; up to 0.5 mile

Approximate hiking time: 30 minutes max, unless you dawdle

Difficulty: Easy

Trail surface: Flat and firm, sometimes grassy

Other trail users: None; no dogs or horses allowed

Best season: Year-round, except when covered with snow or ice

Canine compatibility: Dogs not permitted

Fees and permits: None

Schedule: Closed only when inclement weather closes New-found Gap Road

Maps: TOPO! North Carolina, South Carolina

Trail contacts: Information about trails, camping, road closures, as well as downloadable maps and a "Smokies Trip Planner" are available online under the "Plan Your Visit" part of the park's excellent Web site, www.nps.gov/grsm. The Backcountry Information Office is open 9 a.m. to noon, 865-436-1297.

Finding the trailhead: Driving north from Oconaluftee Visitor Center, these paths are located on the right (east) at 7.4 miles, 11 miles, 13.7 miles, 14.1 miles, and 14.6 miles. Most are marked by small QUIET WALKWAY signs at the parking turnouts.

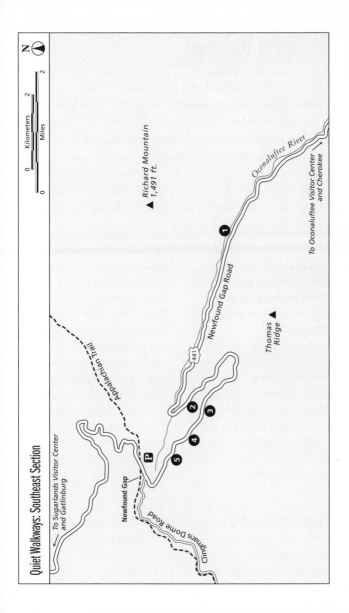

Quiet Walkways: Southeast Section

To Sugarlands Visitor Center and Gatlinburg

Appalachian Trail

Newfound Gap

Clingmans Dome Road

Newfound Gap Road

441

P

▲ Richard Mountain
1,491 ft.

▲ Thomas Ridge

Oconaluftee River

To Oconaluftee Visitor Center and Cherokee

N

Kilometers 2

Miles 2

The Hike

The first Quiet Walkway in this section of the park (at 7.4 miles) isn't highly recommended: It steeply enters the woods, quickly reaching Flats Prong.

The walkway at 11 miles is a long stretch of the old Newfound Gap Road, the earliest paved road across the park that was closed when a more gradual section of the road was built.

The walkway at 13.7 miles runs along a ridge top perpendicular to the road. Turn around when it heads down. The walkway at 14.1 miles dips into the Deep Creek drainage among northern hardwoods at 4,700 feet.

The loftiest and last walkway, at 14.6 miles and just a little more than 1 mile from the Clingmans Dome Road and Newfound Gap, zigzags steeply down along the ridge with occasional views.

10 Oconaluftee River Trail/Mountain Farm Museum

The Mountain Farm Museum may just be a stroll, but combine it with one of the Smokies' best kept secret easy walks, the Oconaluftee River Trail, and you have one of the park's best combinations of scenery and interpretation. It is a masterful meshing of insight into Native Americans and later settlers.

Distance: Up to 3 miles out and back from the Oconaluftee Visitor Center to Cherokee, with shorter out-and-back options from Newfound Gap Road trailheads to the Mountain Farm Museum and a shuttle option from Oconaluftee Visitor Center to Cherokee

Approximate hiking time: 2 hours with 30-minute shortcut options or 1 hour shuttle

Difficulty: Very easy to moderate, depending on length

Trail surface: Grassy at Mountain Farm, lightly graveled road-width path

Other trail users: This is one of the very few trails in the Smokies where dogs and bikes are permitted

Best season: Year-round

Canine compatibility: Dogs are permitted on the Oconaluftee River Trail while on leash—but no dogs are allowed in the Mountain Farm Museum enclosure

Fees and permits: None

Schedule: Year-round. Even when inclement weather closes Newfound Gap Road, this trail can be hiked from the Cherokee trailhead.

Maps: USGS Smokemont and Whittier; TOPO! North Carolina, South Carolina

Trail contacts: Information about trails, camping, road closures, as well as downloadable maps and a "Smokies Trip Planner" are available online under the "Plan Your Visit" part of the park's excellent Web site, www.nps.gov/grsm. The Backcountry Information Office is open 9 a.m. to noon, 865-436-1297.

Special considerations: This hike can be started from a variety of trailheads, making it customizable for different distances and fitness levels.

Finding the trailhead: Park at the Oconaluftee Visitor Center (where restrooms and water are available), at the Cherokee Transit parking area in Cherokee, or at any of three pull-offs between Cherokee and the Oconaluftee Visitor Center on the right side of Newfound Gap Road. From the park boundary at Cherokee, those parking spots are located at 0.3 mile (a turnout at the park entrance sign), 0.5 mile (a parking pull-off), and at 0.7 mile there's a single car parking spot at the start of the Blue Ridge Parkway. To reach that, turn right/northeast from Newfound Gap Road onto the Parkway, turn around at the first overlook, and on the way back to Newfound Gap Road, pull off the Parkway to the right onto roadside gravel just across the bridge from milepost 469. Ocanaluftee Visitor Center trailhead GPS: N35 30.786' / W83 18.398'

The Hike

If you've ever wondered what a hog does when an overspreading oak drops a September acorn into its artfully sited sty, this trail can answer that question.

I may be overly fond of this path, in part because the route suggested combines two separate experiences that aren't linked in other trail publications.

The Mountain Farm Museum is a flat, 0.5-mile wander among a stunning collection of nineteenth-century backcountry farm structures that paint a vivid picture of a settler's life, complete with chickens crowing and pigs grunting. The Oconaluftee River Trail (ORT) leads from the farm to Cherokee—or from Cherokee to the farm. Hiking either way offers a major dose of riverside scenery along with what may be the park's best insight into Cherokee Indian culture.

A half dozen interpretive plaques on the trail explain Cherokee beliefs and respect for the natural world (in English and Cherokee). The signs include evocative illustrations by Cherokee artists that will make you want to visit the tribe's Qualla Arts and Crafts gallery in town. There's a bench at each sign and at other places along the path.

Above the visitor center the river flows narrow and fast along Newfound Gap Road, but along the ORT, the Oconaluftee spreads wide and dances over ledges and around islands. The river starts in one of the East's biggest wilderness areas and the refreshing clean smell of the water matches the emerald green color in a way that defies verbal description.

All along the river there's an open understory of grasses and ferns with many wildflowers, including bee balm and entire trailside borders of jewelweed or touch-me-not (in late August).

One reason the ORT is a good family hike for visitors is that it's very popular with Cherokees as a place to jog or stroll with family. Seeing local Native Americans enjoying their ancestral homeland while you pause to read interpretive signs about Cherokee legend is a rich experience you won't get by stopping at the Bear Trap souvenir shop.

Leave the visitor center's south side and the trail splits; go left (east) to the Mountain Farm Museum and right (southeast) to the Oconaluftee River Trail that skirts the farm. Explore the farm first—the interpretive signs that explain the structures, all gathered in 1950 from throughout the Smokies, also picture many in their original locations. After you've toured the farm, exit past the Apple House near the cornfield and turn left (southeast) on the ORT. The trail follows the farm's fence line, then swings close to the river at the first Cherokee cultural sign.

At 0.7 mile the trail goes under the Blue Ridge Parkway bridge and side steps lead right (south) to a roadside parking slip (one of three places to park along the ORT that permit shorter out-and-back hikes from the roadside to the Mountain Farm Museum and back—the reverse of the direction described here). The trail swings away from the river and at 0.9 mile crosses a small bridge where a right (west) turn up the rooty bank just beyond leads to the second roadside trailhead, this one a designated parking area on Newfound Gap Road. At 1.2 miles from the Mountain Farm Museum, a rock wall leads right (west) to the next roadside trailhead at the park's major entrance sign (the first parking spot reached from Cherokee). The trail then crosses Big Cove Road at 1.3 miles and reaches the sidewalks of Cherokee across from the Cherokee Transit parking area at the reservation boundary at 1.5 miles.

By the way—when the acorn drops into the pig sty, the pig trots right to it!

Options

If you don't want to start at the visitor center, choose the roadside parking area that's right for you and hike out-and-back to the Mountain Farm Museum. From the Cherokee Transit lot the round-trip hike to the museum is 3 miles (the same distance as from the visitor center to Cherokee and back). The round-trip hike to the museum is 2.4 miles from the park entrance sign lot, 1.8 miles from the parking area near the trail bridge (immediately before the sign BLUE RIDGE PARKWAY NEXT RIGHT), and 1.4 miles from the roadside slip at the start of the Blue Ridge Parkway (see "Finding the trailhead" for road directions). From all of these starting points, you begin with Cherokee culture, in a scenic, natural setting, and end with the newcomers.

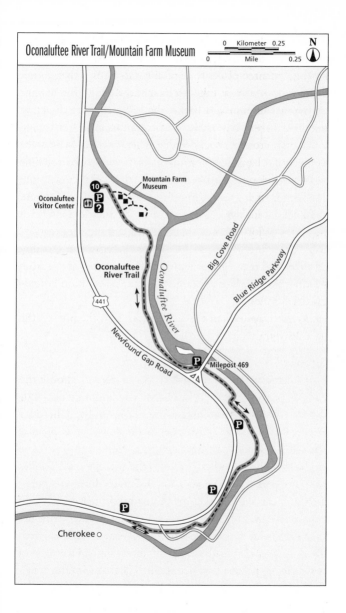

Oconaluftee River Trail/Mountain Farm Museum

Kilometer
0   0.25

Mile
0   0.25

N

Mountain Farm Museum

10

Oconaluftee
Visitor Center

**Oconaluftee
River Trail**

441

Newfound Gap Road

Oconaluftee River

Big Cove Road

Blue Ridge Parkway

Milepost 469

Cherokee

Want to have the entire experience with half the round-trip distance? Leave your car at the Cherokee Transit parking area (directly across from the Oconaluftee River Trailhead in Cherokee) and take the shuttle that runs between Cherokee and Gatlinburg/Pigeon Forge. Get off at the Oconaluftee Visitor Center. The shuttle runs many times daily from May through October (a fee is charged). Stroll through the museum then walk back to your car for a 1.5-mile one-way hike.

Miles and Directions

0.0 Start at the Oconaluftee Visitor Center.

0.7 Pass side steps to the Blue Ridge Parkway.

1.2 Pass the park entrance sign.

1.5 Reach the Cherokee Transit parking area and turnaround point.

3.0 Arrive back at the trailhead at the Oconaluftee Visitor Center.

11 Smokemont Self-Guiding Nature Trail/Smokemont Loop

One of the park's steeper nature trails rises above Smoke-mont Campground, site of one of the Smokies' biggest early twentieth-century logging operations. A few longer options include a loop and a very easy overnighter for beginner backpackers.

Distance: 0.75-mile lollipop loop (nature trail); 6.1-mile loop; 3.6-mile backpacking option

Approximate hiking time: 30 minutes for the nature trail, 3 hours for the loop

Difficulty: Easy for nature trail/moderate for loop

Trail surface: Packed clay soil surface, with a very rooty upper section for the nature trail. For the loop, the hike starts on a gravel road and ends on a steeper forest trail.

Other trail users: The Bradley Fork Trail, Chasteen Creek Trail, and campsite 50 are open to equestrian traffic.

Best season: Spring for wildflowers (on the loop)

Canine compatibility: Dogs not permitted

Fees and permits: None

Schedule: Closed only when inclement weather closes Newfound Gap Road. Smokemont Campground is open year-round.

Maps: USGS Smokemont; TOPO! North Carolina, South Carolina

Trail contacts: Information about trails, camping, road closures, as well as downloadable maps and a "Smokies Trip Planner" are available online under the "Plan Your Visit" part of the park's excellent Web site, www.nps.gov/grsm. The Backcountry Information Office is open 9 a.m. to noon, 865-436-1297. To reserve campsite 50, call the Backcountry Reservation Office (open 8 a.m. to 6 p.m.; 865-436-1231) a month in advance of your first planned day on the trail.

Special considerations: You'll need to reserve a spot in advance at campsite 50 if you plan to do the optional 3.6-mile out-and-back backpacking trip.

Finding the trailhead: From Newfound Gap Road turn right (north) into Smokemont Campground, located 3.2 miles north of Oconaluftee Visitor Center. Cross the river bridge to the T junction and go left. Pass the campground check-in kiosk and not far beyond, turn left and park on the right opposite campsites B31 and B32 (restrooms are available just beyond, on the left, by Campsite B36). To reach the start of the Smokemont Loop, either pass the nature trail and park on the right at an old bridge, or drive farther into the campground and where the D loop splits, take the left fork for sites D20 to D45. Park at the end of the loop near Campsite D32 at the BRADLEY FORK TRAIL sign (restrooms are available near Campsite D29 just south of the trailhead). When you finish the loop hike, you'll need to walk back through the campground to wherever you parked. In winter, with D loop and its restroom closed, the recommended parking spot is near the nature trail at the old bridge, not far from watchful ranger offices near the campground entrance. Nature trail trailhead GPS: N35 33.465' / W83 18.742'

The Hike

The Smokemont Nature Trail starts at a roadside sign and crosses three single log bridges that impart a deep woods Smokies feel. The second bridge spans lively, cacophonous Bradley Fork, and the third crosses a silent, lazy side flow that could almost be another creek in a completely different place. Beyond, the trail slams into a sharp hillside and splits, each side rising steeply to wrap around the knob above.

Go right (north) and the trail undulates up along a very steep side hill overlooking the campground. No flat little loop this: You're immediately up and out of the campground in a place that's suddenly not so tame. An irony, given that the campground occupies the site of an early twentieth-century logging village that denuded the surrounding mountainsides, causing devastating fires and floods. The trail's brochure recounts the destruction and recovery at twelve posts along the way.

The trail climbs to the right then switchbacks left just below the peak of the knob on rooty footing through rhododendron and mountain laurel. When the path slides onto a ridgetop beyond, you'll sniff wood smoke from campfires being drawn through the gap, while right-hand views open up to the high Smokies (with a bench).

Running down the ridge, the trail veers right (north) off the back of the knob, then left (south) through mountain laurel and white pines above the emerging sound of a stream and traffic on Newfound Gap Road. A sign points left (north) on the nature trail where an informal side trail leaves to the right (a connector to the Smokemont Loop Trail). The main nature trail swings left (north) across the lower face of the knob to a right (east) turn leading back across the bridges you started on.

As you drive out of the campground, look right (west) 100 yards from the trailhead to an atmospheric old road bridge. This is old US 441, since rerouted as the more modern Newfound Gap Road, now part of the Smokemont Loop Trail. If you turn right (south) at the informal trail mentioned above, you'll descend to that old road, where a left (east) turn leads across the old bridge. Walk left (north) on the campground road to your car at the trailhead.

The stretch described above is part of the longer 6-mile hike beginning at the campground, the Smokemont Loop. Starting at the end of D loop, pass the gate on the gravel, road-width Bradley Fork Trail and reach the Chasteen Creek Trail on the right (north) at 1.2 miles.

Continue left (northwest) on the Bradley Fork Trail, then head left (west) at 1.7 miles on the Smokemont Loop Trail (the Bradley Fork Trail bears right/north). The Smokemont trail crosses a really long log footbridge, then makes a stiff 2-mile climb. Still climbing as it crosses to the west side of the ridge, the trail swings hard left (south) around one of the southernmost peaks of Richland Mountain. Dipping to a grassy little gap between summits (at about 3.5 miles), the trail starts its descent within earshot of Newfound Gap Road. Nearing the campground you might see Bradley Cemetery off to the right (south). Stay on the main trail and a little farther on, at about 5.4 miles, a side path leads back to the site, one of the largest cemeteries in the Smokies. Not far beyond, old US 441 leads into the campground. Back at your car on D loop, it's a 6.1-mile hike.

Option

For an easy backpacking trip, start the Smokemont Loop hike as above, following the Bradley Fork Trail. Turn right (north) at 1.2 miles on the Chasteen Creek Trail and continue another 0.1 mile along the stream to campsite 50. You must have a reservation for campsite 50. Start early and after setting up camp, Chasteen Creek Cascades is only 0.6 mile farther—the perfect afternoon day hike before dinner. Total roundtrip: just 3.6 miles.

Smokemont Self-Guiding Nature Trail and Loop

Kilometer
0   0.5
Mile
0   0.5

N

Bradley

Fork   Trail

Chasteen Creek Trail

Campsite 50

Bradley Fork

Richland Mountain

Smokemont Loop

Oconaluftee River

441

Smokemont Self-Guiding Nature Trail

Bradley Cemetery

11

Smokemont Campground

P

P

Newfound Gap Road

Miles and Directions

Smokemont Loop

0.0   Start at the D Loop trailhead on the Bradley Fork Trail.

1.2   Chasteen Creek Trail goes right (north); stay left (northwest) on Bradley Fork Trail.

1.7   Take the Smokemont Loop Trail to the left (west) and across the long bridge.

5.4   Arrive at Bradley Cemetery.

5.6   Return to the campground, then go left (north) to the end of D Loop.

6.1   Arrive back at the Bradley Fork trailhead.

12 Ferguson Cabin

A best-kept secret, this entry point to the national park near Maggie Valley permits an easy hike to the highest log cabin in the Smokies.

Distance: 2.8-mile lollipop; 1.8 miles out and back to the cabin
Approximate hiking time: 2 hours
Difficulty: Easy
Trail surface: Gravel forest road, meadow path, and hardened forest trail
Other trail users: Some equestrian traffic near the Cataloochee Divide Trail
Best season: Spring through fall
Canine compatibility: Dogs not permitted
Fees and permits: None
Schedule: See "Special considerations" below
Maps: USGS Dellwood; TOPO! North Carolina, South Carolina
Trail contact: Appalachian Highlands Science Learning Center; (828) 926-6251
Special considerations: The Purchase Knob environmental education center is a residence for scientists studying the park and is not equipped to cater to drop-in visitors. Please park outside the gate; do not block traffic, or otherwise interfere with the facility's work.

Finding the trailhead: From Asheville, North Carolina, go west on I-40. Take exit 20 and travel south on US 276 toward Maggie Valley. In 2.8 miles, turn right (west) onto Grindstone Road, then right (west) on Hemphill Road. Drive 3 miles. Pass the entrance to the Swag Country Inn on the left (west), and park 0.8 mile beyond near the gate for the Purchase Knob environmental education center. Do not block the road. Hike up the road to a meadow, where you'll see a trail sign to the cabin. GPS: N35 34 22.155' / W83 4 34.658'

The Hike

The circa-1870s John Love Ferguson Cabin, the Smokies' highest, sits 5,000 feet above sea level. It's accessible from the gate of the Appalachian Highlands Science Learning Center, one of the five such centers established in national parks in 2001. Once the estate of Voit Gilmore and Kathryn McNeil, the 530-acre Purchase Knob tract was donated to the park in 2000 and is the Smokies' largest private gift. The former summer home is now a facility where school and other groups come to help scientists in residence with park research.

The easy, 2.8-mile lollipop loop starts near the learning center's gate. Walk up the scenic woods road and go left (west) across the meadow at a trail sign to Ferguson Cabin. Explore the inside.

Return to your car for a 1.8-mile out-and-back hike, or continue the loop by exiting the cabin and turning right (west) uphill into the woods along the stream. You'll cross the creek, and reach a junction. A left (west) turn leads onto a connector trail to the Cataloochee Divide Trail, but turn right (east) to return to the meadow sign and your car.

Option

The Swag, the mile-high country inn you passed on your drive to Purchase Knob, is a hiker's destination (www.theswag.com). From April through August, experts and naturalists engage guests with interpretive programs and guided hikes. A tree trunk holds hiking staffs (with a wooden name medallion for each guest), inviting you to grab one and stride off on a hike. Guests often visit Ferguson Cabin and nearby Hemphill Bald, a spectacular, hard-to-reach Smokies summit that is an easy hike from the inn. The Swag has a

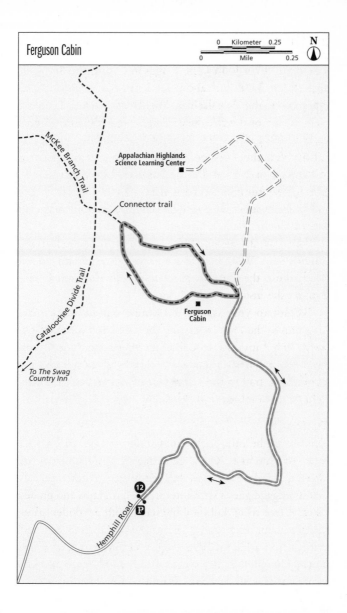

Ferguson Cabin

McKee Branch Trail

Appalachian Highlands
Science Learning Center

Connector trail

Cataloochee Divide Trail

Ferguson
Cabin

To The Swag
Country Inn

12

P

Hemphill Road

0 Kilometer 0.25
0 Mile 0.25

N

national reputation for fine food and lodging, so staying in one of the inn's magical collection of cottages and lodges built from ancient Appalachian cabins will not be cheap.

Miles and Directions

0.0 Start from the gate by hiking up the gravel road.

0.9 Reach the Ferguson Cabin.

1.9 Complete the loop from the meadow and cabin; turn right (south) on the road back to your car.

2.8 Arrive back at the trailhead.

13 The Boogerman Trail

This hike mixes multiple bridge crossings on Caldwell Fork Trail, one of the Smokies best stream hikes, with historic ruins and sights of the Smokies' inspiring virgin forests along the Boogerman Trail.

Distance: 7.4-mile loop (with options for out-and-back hikes and a 9.6-mile backpacking trip)

Approximate hiking time: 5 hours

Difficulty: Moderate for the loop, easy for an out-and-back trek. More challenging for backpacking, mostly due to distance and possible muck.

Trail surface: Typical forest path for Boogerman. Mixed horse/hiker use on the Caldwell Fork Trail makes for some mud and rocks.

Other trail users: Horses are permitted on the Caldwell Fork Trail.

Best season: Drier weather periods in winter and fall

Canine compatibility: Dogs not permitted

Fees and permits: None

Schedule: Heavy snow might complicate access on the Cataloochee area's unpaved roads.

Maps: USGS Cove Creek Gap and Dellwood; TOPO! North Carolina, South Carolina

Trail contacts: You won't need to reserve campsite 41, but you will need a backcountry camping permit to spend the night. Call the Backcountry Reservation Office (open 8 a.m. to 6 p.m.; 865-436-1231) a month in advance of your first planned day on the trail. Information about trails, camping, road closures, as well as downloadable maps and a "Smokies Trip Planner" are available online under the "Plan Your Visit" part of the park's excellent Web site, www.nps.gov/grsm. The Backcountry Information Office is open 9 a.m. to noon, 865-436-1297.

Special considerations: A hiking staff, trekking poles, and high-top boots might make it easier to avoid muddy spots if you hike in wetter weather.

Finding the trailhead: From Asheville, North Carolina, take I-40 to exit 20, and go south toward Maggie Valley on US 276. Take the first right on Cove Creek Road, heading north, and go 7.4 miles to a left turn, on the road to Cataloochee, where the road changes from gravel to pavement. The Caldwell Fork Trail begins on the left (south) in 3.1 miles at a small roadside pullout just beyond the Cataloochee Campground (where restrooms are available in season). GPS: N35 37 53.504' / W83 05.283'

The Hike

The Caldwell Fork Trail bisects a huge drainage, where a variety of trails create diverse day and overnight circuit hikes. A loop using the Boogerman Trail is one of the best, for a 7.4-mile circuit. Leave the tiny parking spot beside the road on Caldwell Fork Trail, and cross what may be the park's biggest single log bridge, the first of twenty that lead up this trail. This may be your first photo—it's a great downstream nature shot, not to mention one of your hiking companions firmly grasping the bridge railing!

At 0.8 mile, head left (southeast) on the Boogerman Trail. It winds away and above the Caldwell Fork, eventually returning at 4.7 miles after rising along the west flank of the prominent Cataloochee Divide. Along the way you'll cross small bridges and easily hop streams on a refreshingly "hikers only" path that undulates through tall timber, the result of Robert "Booger" Palmer's refusal to cut the big trees on his stream-laced property. You'll pass through "Booger's" farm site; be on the lookout later for an especially impressive stone wall and then others, less well-preserved. As you near Caldwell Fork Trail look left (south) for the last remnants of Carson Messer's cabin. Turn right (north), traveling back along Caldwell Fork to your car.

The Boogerman Trail

Kilometer
0   1

Mile
0   1

N

Messer Barn

P

Cataloochee Campground

Cataloochee Road

Palmer Creek

Palmer Chapel

Caldwell House

Rough Fork

Caldwell Fork Trail

Big Fork Ridge Trail

Boogerman Trail

Farm Site

Caldwell Fork Trail

McKee Branch Trail

Campsite 41

Hemphill Bald Trail

Cataloochee Divide Trail

Options

The easiest hike in this area is a simple out and back on the Caldwell Fork Trail. As Boogerman hikers discover, views are awesome along the stream—and from the bridges. Just turn around when you want.

If the weather's dry and horse traffic hasn't made the trail too muddy, backpackers can make an easy overnighter out of this gradual streamside walk to the Smokies' designated campsite 41, 4.8 miles from the parking area. On the way along the Caldwell Fork Trail you pass both entrances to the Boogerman Trail (on the left/east), the Big Fork Ridge Trail at 3.1 miles (on the right/northwest), the McKee Branch Trail at 3.2 miles on the left/southeast (site of the Caldwell Fork community and its grist mill), and Hemphill Bald Trail on the left (southeast) at 4.7 miles. Cross the final bridge over Caldwell Fork to reach campsite 41. Take a rest, but consider going a ways beyond the campsite. A sign to the right (north) soon directs you to "Big Poplars," a grove of towering, centuries-old tulip poplars. These awesome giants were spared by Cataloochee resident John Caldwell. Above that, the hardwood and hemlock forest becomes impressively mature. Backtrack for a 9.6-mile overnighter.

Miles and Directions

0.0 Start by crossing the long log bridge on the Caldwell Fork Trail.

0.8 Turn left (southeast) from the Caldwell Fork Trail onto the Boogerman Trail.

4.7 Turn right (north) on the Caldwell Fork Trail.

6.6 Pass the first Boogerman Trail junction.

7.4 Arrive back at the trailhead.

14 Big Creek

A waterfall, swimming holes, and a scenic backcountry campsite make this a temptingly multifaceted day or overnight hike.

Distance: 4 miles out and back to the waterfall; an out-and-back backpack option of 10.6 miles

Approximate hiking time: 1 hour to Mouse Creek Falls

Difficulty: Easy to moderate

Trail surface: Gradual old railroad grade

Other trail users: Equestrians, but it's easy to avoid evidence of their "passing"

Best season: Year-round, but summer if the stream tempts

Canine compatibility: Dogs not permitted

Fees and permits: None

Schedule: Heavy snow might complicate access on the Deep Creek area's unpaved roads.

Maps: USGS Waterville, Cove Creek Gap, Luftee Knob; TOPO! North Carolina, South Carolina

Trail contacts: To reserve campsite 37, call the Backcountry Reservation Office (open 8 a.m. to 6 p.m.; 865-436-1231) a month in advance of your first planned day on the trail. Information about trails, camping, road closures, as well as downloadable maps and a "Smokies Trip Planner" are available online under the "Plan Your Visit" part of the park's excellent Web site, www.nps.gov/grsm. The Backcountry Information Office is open 9 a.m. to noon, 865-436-1297.

Finding the trailhead: From I-40 near the Tennessee/North Carolina state line, take exit 451 (in Tennessee) for Waterville. Turn back under the interstate to cross, then parallel, the Pigeon River past Mountain Mama's store/eatery. About 100 yards later come to a crossroads in the village of Mount Sterling. Go straight through the intersection; the Big Creek Ranger Station is 0.2 mile ahead on the right (west). The Big Creek Picnic Area trailhead (where restrooms are

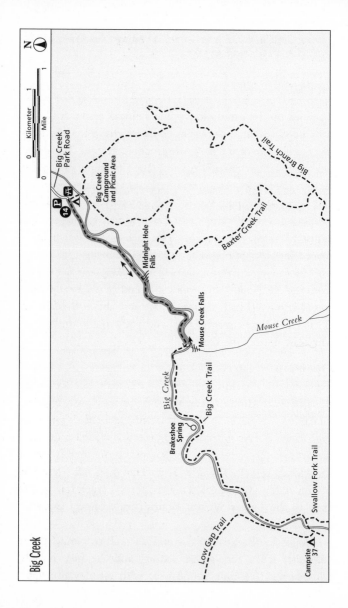

Big Creek

available) is another 0.6 mile beyond, on the right (southwest). GPS:
N35 45 06.793' / W83 06.583'

The Hike

Take off up the gated old logging railroad grade. It bumps
up abruptly at first, then rises easily its entire length along
Big Creek, one of the park's most scenic streams. The grade
lies on the right (north) side of Big Creek on this lower
section of the trail. At 1.4 miles, Midnight Hole is a perfect,
and deep, swim spot. You'll need a hot day—the Smokies
are not known for warm water. Luckily, this dipping place is
at just 2,000 feet in elevation. (The park's more forbiddingly
named Icewater Spring is at almost 6,000 feet.)

Mouse Creek Falls cascades spectacularly into Big Creek
from the left (south) at 2 miles (the end of the easy 4-mile
round-trip day hike). At the bridge just above the falls, at
2,358 feet, there's another pool and you cross to the left, or
southeast side, of the creek.

Option

To make this a backpacking trip, continue on the Big Creek
Trail beyond Mouse Creek Falls. At just less than 3 miles,
Brakeshoe Spring is on the left (south), named during logging railroad days when a brakeshoe was placed under the
rivulet to catch water. The creek winds more sharply above
the spring, and the Swallow Fork Trail goes left (south) at
5.1 miles. The Big Creek Trail crosses the creek for the last
time to the Lower Walnut Bottom backcountry campsite
37, at 5.3 miles.

Beginning backpackers would do well to consider this
campsite. It's a very scenic setting, and the hike is only
a moderate 10.6-mile round-trip, with an elevation gain

of 1,000 feet (also doable for more energetic day hikers). This is a popular campsite, in part because it accommodates twenty backpackers but not horse campers. A reservation is required, so book as far in advance as you can.

Miles and Directions

0.0 Start by following the old railroad grade along Big Creek.

1.4 Arrive at Midnight Hole.

2.0 Reach Mouse Creek Falls. This is the turnaround point for the 4-mile round-trip day hike.

Backpacking overnight option

2.8 Pass Brakeshoe Spring on the left (south).

5.1 Swallow Fork Trail goes left (south), stay straight to the campsite.

5.3 Arrive at campsite 37. Spend the night, then return as you came.

10.6 Arrive back at the trailhead.

Southwest Section

15 Spruce-Fir Self-Guiding Nature Trail

This 0.5-mile nature trail wanders the whispering lush evergreens of a Canadian zone forest. It also showcases a microcosm of the environmental factors that are destroying the world's high-elevation woodlands.

Distance: 0.5-mile loop

Approximate hiking time: 30 minutes

Difficulty: Easy

Trail surface: Smooth forest floor

Other trail users: None; no dogs or horses allowed

Best season: Summer for lushness; winter for stark landscapes

Canine compatibility: Dogs not permitted

Fees and permits: None

Schedule: The Clingmans Dome Road is closed in winter, from Dec 1 through Mar 31 (when cross-country skiers rule the road)

Maps: USGS Clingmans Dome; TOPO! North Carolina, South Carolina

Trail contacts: Information about trails, camping, road closures, as well as downloadable maps and a "Smokies Trip Planner" are available online under the "Plan Your Visit" part of the park's excellent Web site, www .nps.gov/grsm. The Backcountry Information Office is open 9 a.m. to noon, 865-436-1297.

Special considerations: Pull into this tiny trailhead going east on the way back from Clingmans Dome.

Other: If you reach the Smokies from the Blue Ridge Parkway, notice the interpretive information about forest decline evident at Mount Mitchell and Richland Balsam, both featured in FalconGuides' *Best Easy Day Hikes Blue Ridge Parkway.*

Finding the trailhead: The Spruce-Fir Self-Guiding Nature Trail is on the Clingmans Dome Road, 2.6 miles from the junction with Newfound Gap Road, 18.4 miles from the Oconaluftee Visitor Center, and 15.8 miles from the Sugarlands Visitor Center. GPS: N35 35 741' / W83 27.519'

The Hike

Early on, it was known that the Fraser fir in this high forest was being decimated by the balsam woolly adelgid, a pest introduced into the United States around 1900. But that didn't explain the decline of the red spruces that also grow here. More recent studies suggest damage to both species by acid rain—highly acidic precipitation that upsets the pH balance of the soil, freeing heavy metals that inhibit a tree's ability to ingest nutrients. Another significant factor also has been discovered: ozone. Research suggests that, like the smog trapped in cities, airborne pollution from major utilities and industries located upwind leads to startlingly high ozone levels on southern summits. Such pollution, often contained in cloud caps as acidic as vinegar, burns the needles of firs, dramatically inhibiting the growth and survival of evergreens already fighting a severe climate. The result is that stark tree skeletons stand here and elsewhere in the park, tall and gray in ghostlike groves.

One of the natural forces destroying these high elevation forests is wind. When openings appear as weakened trees are felled, healthier trees suffer the fuller force of the wind. Near the end of this loop, you'll see one spruce that fell despite a huge root system.

The taller trees may be dying, but you'll see younger trees springing up before suffering themselves. Use your

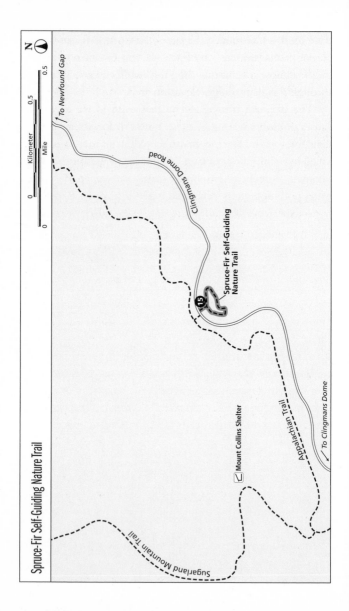

Spruce-Fir Self-Guiding Nature Trail

N

To Newfound Gap

Clingmans Dome Road

Spruce-Fir Self-Guiding Nature Trail

15

Mount Collins Shelter

Appalachian Trail

To Clingmans Dome

Sugarland Mountain Trail

Kilometer

Mile

0   0.5

0   0.5

time on this trail to notice many other spruce-fir forest species of plants, animals, and birds—if you can take your eyes off the almost continuous "bog log" walkway you'll traverse through this damp, high elevation area.

The ultimate irony may be that even as we argue the causes of global warming, these northern forests, so dependent for survival on the South's coldest climate, are being killed by simple air pollution. That same pollution can make hiking a little harder on hazy days, and the park indeed issues pollution alerts. There's no better place in the Smokies to experience the unfolding tragedy of what we're doing to our planet.

16 Clingmans Dome

The Smokies'—and Tennessee's—highest peak (6,643 feet) is more than just another chance to add to your life list of grandiose summits to conquer. The vista is astounding when the weather's right.

Distance: 1.0 mile out and back
Approximate hiking time: 1.5 hours
Difficulty: Moderate
Trail surface: Paved
Other trail users: None
Best season: November is the clearest nonwinter month
Canine compatibility: Dogs not permitted
Fees and permits: None
Schedule: The Clingmans Dome Road is closed in winter, from Dec 1 through Mar 31 (when cross country skiers rule the road).

Maps: USGS Clingmans Dome; TOPO! Tennessee, Kentucky
Trail contacts: Information about trails, camping, road closures, as well as downloadable maps and a "Smokies Trip Planner" are available online under the "Plan Your Visit" part of the park's excellent Web site, www .nps.gov/grsm. The Backcountry Information Office is open 9 a.m. to noon, 865-436-1297.
Special considerations: Get going early on this hike. It'll be clearer, and the parking lot will be emptier.

Finding the trailhead: The Clingmans Dome parking area is on the Clingmans Dome Road, 7.6 miles west of the junction with Newfound Gap Road. Restrooms are in the parking lot. GPS: N35 33.389'/W83 29.721'

The Hike

Grab that restroom break at the parking lot, then take the steep paved path past rest benches. You'll pass a connector

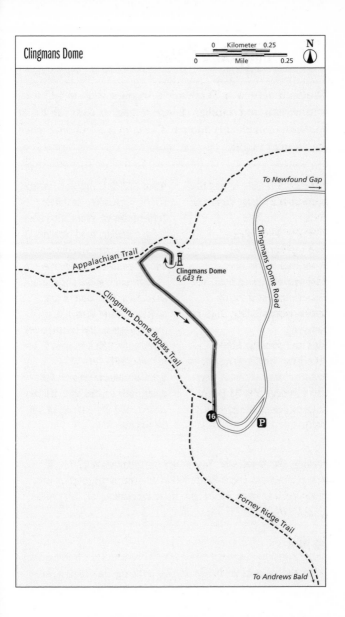

Clingmans Dome

0   Kilometer   0.25

0   Mile   0.25

N

To Newfound Gap

Appalachian Trail

Clingmans Dome Road

Clingmans Dome
6,643 ft.

Clingmans Dome Bypass Trail

16

P

Forney Ridge Trail

To Andrews Bald

to the AT on the left (north), then reach and ascend the tower that corkscrews its way above the peak. The increasingly decimated evergreen forest here (take the Spruce-Fir Nature Trail to learn more about the park's ecological problems) affords even better views than when a tower was first needed to reach above the trees.

Winter offers the best views from Clingmans Dome, but the road is closed December to March due to predictably heavy snowfalls. Only cross-country skiers willing to ski 14 miles round-trip (or backpackers on the Appalachian Trail) are likely to see the broadest curve of the Earth.

Nevertheless, the high southern Appalachians routinely receive summer cold front incursions that redeem the mountains' reputation for the region's coolest, and clearest, summer weather. Use your clearest day for this hike—or not. There is definitely something to be said for exploring the inside of a cloud at nearly 7,000 feet. You'll remember the damp, cool, dripping realm of Clingmans Dome even if you can't see down to Cherokee.

Miles and Directions

0.0 Start in the parking lot.

0.5 Reach the top of Clingmans Dome.

1.0 Arrive back at the trailhead.

17 Juney Whank Falls

This is a nice mini–waterfall walk for kids and those with only a little time.

Distance: 0.7-mile loop
Approximate hiking time: 45 minutes
Difficulty: Easy, with a moderate climb and steeper descent
Trail surface: Mostly road grade or packed trail
Other trail users: You may see equestrians along the bridle trail portion of this hike
Best season: Best in spring or after a rain, which increases the flow in this small stream
Canine compatibility: Dogs not permitted
Fees and permits: None
Schedule: Year-round
Maps: USGS Bryson City; TOPO! North Carolina, South Carolina

Trail contacts: Information about trails, camping, road closures, as well as downloadable maps and a "Smokies Trip Planner" are available online under the "Plan Your Visit" part of the park's excellent Web site, www .nps.gov/grsm. The Backcountry Information Office is open 9 a.m. to noon, 865-436-1297.
Special considerations: You won't need to cope with a busy parking area if you camp at Deep Creek Campground (especially at campsites 30 and up), where it's easy to step up onto Galbraith Creek Road. Go left (northwest) across the bridge, and you can hike both to Juney Whank Falls and on the Deep Creek Loop.

Finding the trailhead: Take any of a number of well-signed routes north from downtown Bryson City into the park. After passing the cluster of businesses at the park boundary, pass the Deep Creek Campground and the picnic area (where restrooms are avilable in season), both on the right (east), and turn left into the parking area as you reach a bridge on the right/east (the Galbraith Creek Road). The road ahead is a circular drop-off point. Take the gravel grade at the upper left (north) end of the lot. GPS: N35 27.854' / W83 26.064'

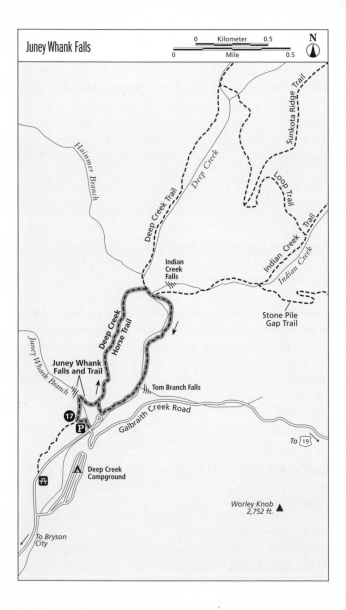

Juney Whank Falls

Kilometer

Mile

N

Hammer Branch

Deep Creek Trail

Deep Creek

Sunkota Ridge Trail

Loop Trail

Indian Creek Trail

Indian Creek Falls

Indian Creek

Stone Pile Gap Trail

Deep Creek Horse Trail

Juney Whank Falls and Trail

Tom Branch Falls

Juney Whank Branch

17

P

Galbraith Creek Road

To 19

Deep Creek Campground

Worley Knob 2,752 ft.

To Bryson City

The Hike

Climb the wide road grade up and left (north) from the parking lot to a junction with the Deep Creek Horse Trail. The bridle trail descends left and rises right: Turn right (south) up the wood steps, and shortly turn right (northeast) again at the FALLS sign. The trail dips down nice rock steps and crosses a scenic bridge below the falls, where you'll find an embedded bench. Just past the bridge, there's a perfect rock seat at the base of the falls. You could almost picture a Romantic poet perched there pondering. Near the falls, THIS IS NOT A TRAIL signs are actually embedded in some bootleg paths that might mislead the inexperienced.

The trail rises beyond the falls and rejoins the bridle trail that crossed the stream above the cascade. Turn right (east) on the bridle trail junction beyond the falls. This area is very well-signed and easy to follow. Just ahead, turn right (southeast) again off the bridle trail at another sign and descend a steep, mountain laurel-sheltered gully. Don't fear—what once was a steep ditch has been wonderfully tamed. A raised graveled tread with steps on the left isolates a rainfall course on the right, with water breaks to foil erosion. If you're not a trail expert, this is an artful solution to an otherwise treacherously erosion-prone piece of path!

At the bottom—and more signs—turn right (southwest) on the Deep Creek Trail, and head back to the parking lot.

Miles and Directions

0.0 Start on the road grade.
0.1 Reach the bridle trail junction and go up the wood steps.
0.3 Arrive at Juney Whank Falls.
0.7 Arrive back at the trailhead.

18 Deep Creek Loop

This truly great, longer circuit hike is also the park's easiest (no doubt handicapped accessible) walk to a spectacular waterfall, Tom Branch Falls, not to mention Indian Creek Falls and a tubing run or swimming hole excursion on pristine Deep Creek.

Distance: 4.2-mile lollipop with a 3.4-mile out-and-back option

Approximate hiking time: 2 to 3 hours

Difficulty: Easy to moderate

Trail surface: Gravel road grades and firm, packed-soil forest trails

Other trail users: You may see equestrians along portions of this hike. Some trail users may be swimsuit-wearing, tube-toting river runners, at least on the lowest section. And mountain bikers are permitted to ride to the upper stream bridge on the Deep Creek Trail.

Best season: Best after a rain for the waterfalls; in the off-season for more solitude in this popular multiuse area; and at the height of summer on a weekday to film your own outdoor action commercial

Canine compatibility: Dogs are permitted on leash.

Fees and permits: None

Schedule: Year-round

Maps: USGS Bryson City; TOPO! North Carolina, South Carolina

Trail contacts: You won't need to reserve campsite 60, but you will need a backcountry camping permit. Call the Backcountry Reservation Office (open 8 a.m. to 6 p.m.; 865-436-1231) a month in advance of your first planned day on the trail. Information about trails, camping, road closures, as well as downloadable maps and a "Smokies Trip Planner" are available online under the "Plan Your Visit" part of the park's excellent Web site, www .nps.gov/grsm. The Backcountry Information Office is open 9 a.m. to noon, 865-436-1297.

Special considerations: You won't have to cope with a busy parking area if you camp at Deep Creek Campground (especially at campsites 30 and up), where it's easy to step up onto Galbraith Creek Road. Go left (northwest) across the bridge, and take the trail to the right (north).

Finding the trailhead: Take any of a number of well-signed routes north from downtown Bryson City into the park. After passing the cluster of businesses at the park boundary, pass the Deep Creek Campground and the picnic area, both on the right (east), and turn left (northeast) into the parking area. A bridge is on the right/east (Galbraith Creek Road). The road ahead (northeast) is a circular drop-off point. A restroom is available year-round at a picnic pavilion on the left before the trailhead. GPS: N35 27.854' / W83 26.064'

The Hike

Just driving in to the Deep Creek area conveys an important Smokies' impression—these summits may not tower like the Tetons, but you sense that there's a vast wildland ahead that stretches ridge after ridge beyond the park boundary. This hike takes you a ways into that forest.

Head off up the level road grade along the wide, green, and pristine Deep Creek as it flows from the heart of the Smokies. Soon, the sound of the stream rises to a higher pitch and as you amble up to five benches on the riverside . . . there's awesome Tom Branch Falls plummeting into the water on the opposite side of Deep Creek. The road continues along the stream past more benches, and then turns right (east) to cross a bridge. There's a great view of a favorite tubing rapid above the bridge, and from benches across the stream where the road surges more steeply and above the creek. At 0.7 mile, the Indian Creek Trail veers right (east) from the Deep Creek Trail at a sign prohibiting tubing above that point.

Go right (east) on the Indian Creek Trail, and in just a few hundred feet, a side trail descends left (north) to scenic Indian Creek Falls (a 1.4-mile round-trip from the parking area). Continuing on the Indian Creek Trail across another bridge, you'll pass Stone Pile Gap Trail as it drops right (southeast) at 1.2 miles. Beyond, the road grade rises with the river above rhododendron-covered stream banks into a drier forest. Turn left (northwest) on the Loop Trail at 1.5 miles. After a level stretch the trail rises steeply up and left (south) to crest at the Sunkota Ridge at 2.0 miles. If anything the trail drops more steeply off the other side. As you pass a massive white oak, the sound of Deep Creek comes from below.

The trail levels and rejoins the Deep Creek Trail at a T junction at 2.5 miles. To the right (north), the old logging railroad appears trail-like on its way past campsite 60 (a gradual 5.2-mile-round trip for an easy backpack from the trailhead). You will need a reservation to use campsite 60. Turning left (southwest), the gravel road crosses a bridge (the upper limit of mountain bike access). This is a great spot for a dip in Deep Creek. Step down beside the bridge, where there's an old spring box, and the pool below a little rapid must be 15 feet deep.

The trail drops steeply at only one point on its way to another bridge and back to the Indian Creek Trail junction at 3.5 miles. From the junction it's another 0.7 mile back to your car for a 4.2-mile hike.

Option
The Deep Creek Trail, from the trailhead to the swimming hole by the bridge, is 3.4 miles out and back.

Deep Creek Loop

Kilometer 0 0.5

Mile 0 0.5

N

Hammer Branch

Sunkota Ridge Trail

Deep Creek

Deep Creek Trail

Loop Trail

Indian Creek Trail

Indian Creek

Indian Creek Falls

Stone Pile Gap Trail

Deep Creek Horse Trail

Juney Whank Branch

Juney Whank Falls and Trail

Tom Branch Falls

P 18

Galbraith Creek Road

To 19

Deep Creek Campground

Worley Knob 2,752 ft.

To Bryson City

Miles and Directions

0.0 Start by heading up the Deep Creek Trail.

0.2 Reach Tom Branch Falls.

0.7 Reach the junction with the Indian Creek Trail and go right (east).

1.5 Go left (northwest) on the Loop Trail.

2.5 Turn left (southwest), heading back on the Deep Creek Trail.

3.5 Pass the Indian Creek Trail junction.

4.2 Arrive back at the trailhead.

Northwest Section

19 Cove Hardwoods Nature Trail

Here you'll find one of the park's best places to savor the towering grandeur of the old-growth cove hardwood forests that were so characteristic of the virgin Smokies. This must-see trail is the essential Smokies in one short, inspiring hike.

Distance: 1-mile lollipop

Approximate hiking time: 1 hour

Difficulty: Easy to moderate

Trail surface: Even forest path with paved steep sections

Other trail users: None; no dogs or horses allowed

Best season: April's great for carpets of spring flowers and views to the still leafless tops of soaring trees. Summer is best for the deep shade of a cathedral grove.

Canine compatibility: Dogs not permitted

Fees and permits: None

Schedule: Closed only when inclement weather closes Newfound Gap Road

Maps: USGS Mount Le Conte; TOPO! Tennessee, Kentucky

Trail contacts: Information about trails, camping, road closures, as well as downloadable maps and a "Smokies Trip Planner" are available online under the "Plan Your Visit" part of the park's excellent Web site, www .nps.gov/grsm. The Backcountry Information Office is open 9 a.m. to noon, 865-436-1297.

Special considerations: The self-guiding brochure for this trail is particularly worth purchasing— it's available at the trailhead dispenser and at the park's visitor center.

Finding the trailhead: From Newfound Gap Road turn east into the Chimneys Picnic Area, located 8.6 miles north of Newfound Gap and 4.6 miles south of the Sugarlands Visitor Center. Pull into the first parking slip on the right (south), below the trailhead sign and steps. The picnic area's first picturesque stone restroom is to the left and just downhill. GPS: N35 38.193' / W83 29.529'

The Hike

The Chimneys Picnic Area and this nature trail serve up the "forest primeval" of stereotype. Not every unlogged forest appears "virgin" in the towering way found here. This perfect ecosystem of heavy rain and deep, rich soils permits deciduous species such as beech, yellow buckeye, red maple, basswood, yellow birch, and coniferous hemlocks to reach record proportions of grandeur in height, circumference, and age (as old as 500 years).

Up the timber-framed steps past a group picnic site, the trail splits: take a right. The trail rises to the east above the sounds of Newfound Gap Road. Near post #5 there's a huge old hemlock felled beside the trail, with its annual rings ripe for counting. The new timber-boxed steps continue as you rise into a broad cove at 0.25 mile, then into a drainage. Swing back and forth across a stream on old-fashioned stone and concrete bridging from an earlier era. The open understory is nothing but wildflowers.

The trail leads left (southwest) of the stream, and more directly up the cove from former fields and a smaller, selectively harvested forest into unlogged old growth. After a long stretch of old concrete tread near post #9, at about 0.3 mile, the trees rise to appear much like the climax forest that so impressed the earliest Appalachian explorers—and was later almost eradicated by early twentieth-century logging companies.

At post #12, you could pinch a nerve in your neck trying to see the very tops of these trees. You'd need a family of tree huggers to express affection for this one, a yellow buckeye, one of the biggest at more than 12 feet in diameter. This is the top of the loop. If you look uphill, you can

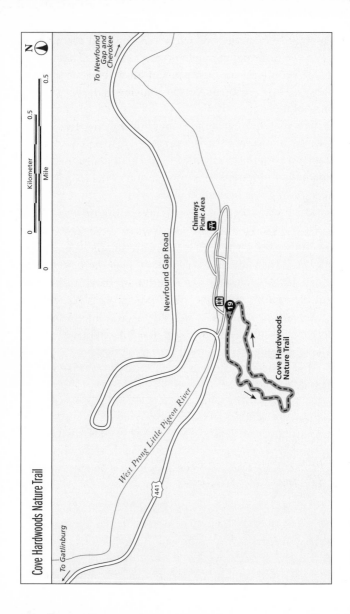

Cove Hardwoods Nature Trail

N

Kilometer
0   0.5

Mile
0   0.5

To Newfound
Gap and
Cherokee

Newfound Gap Road

Chimneys
Picnic Area

19

Cove Hardwoods
Nature Trail

West Prong Little Pigeon River

441

To Gatlinburg

imagine the towering trees marching upward for miles—and they once did throughout the Smokies. The widely spaced trees dominate their patch of soil and reach for every ray of sunlight available. An open, uncluttered, parklike setting lies below.

The trail dips steeply from here into a drier forest, past benches, on a graveled, rocky path. The trail eventually veers right, out of the drainage, at about 0.5 mile, just above your earlier trail and back to the closing of the loop and the picnic area.

Many places in the southern Appalachians once sheltered impressive stands such as these. Today, those that remain are few and far between. This is one of the most accessible. Elsewhere in the Smokies, consider hiking the Cosby Self-Guiding Nature Trail if you're in the northeast part of the park. If a future trip takes you to Nantahala National Forest in western North Carolina, the Joyce Kilmer Memorial Forest is another such forest trail (see FalconGuides' *Hiking North Carolina*).

Miles and Directions

- **0.0** Start by heading up the timber-framed steps.
- **0.2** Travel on an old-style concrete path amid streams and wildflowers.
- **0.4** Reach the top of the loop amid towering trees.
- **1.0** Arrive back at the trailhead.

20 Chimney Tops Trail

This is one of the Smokies' true peak experiences. Great views and exhilarating exposure are both found at the top of this rocky summit. There's also a side trip on the Road Prong Trail that follows the remnants of the park's oldest Native American trail and first transmountain road as it rises toward the peaks.

Distance: 4 miles out and back; plus up to 6.6 miles out-and-back Road Prong options

Approximate hiking time: 2-3 hours

Difficulty: More challenging

Trail surface: Road-width and rocky; includes a rock scramble at the top

Other trail users: None; no dogs or horses allowed

Best season: Spring, when the peak stands above lower lime-green mountainsides; and late fall. Winter can create tricky footing on the rocky summit.

Canine compatibility: Dogs not permitted

Fees and permits: None

Schedule: Closed only when inclement weather closes Newfound Gap Road.

Maps: USGS Mount Le Conte; TOPO! Tennessee, Kentucky

Trail contacts: Information about trails, camping, road closures, as well as downloadable maps and a "Smokies Trip Planner" are available online under the "Plan Your Visit" part of the park's excellent Web site, www .nps.gov/grsm. The Backcountry Information Office is open 9 a.m. to noon, 865-436-1297.

Special considerations: This is one of only a few hikes in this book that is not easy, but was selected because it's one of the shortest, high-adventure hikes. Do not undertake this trail lightly, but it is often hiked by well-equipped, motivated novices in good shape. That, of course, makes this a very popular path. Go early, during the week, and in the off-season if passing lanes on trails aren't your style.

Finding the trailhead: The Chimney Tops parking area is on Newfound Gap Road, 7.1 miles south of the Sugarlands Visitor Center, 2.5 miles south of the Chimneys Picnic Area (closest available restrooms), and 22 miles north of the Oconaluftee Visitor Center. GPS: N35 38.146' / W83 28.195'

The Hike

This popular trail launches a wide and graded trail down to a bridge over Walker Camp Prong. It's uphill from there, and not far beyond you'll cross another bridge, this time over Road Prong. Together, these streams scour the valley below as the West Prong of the Little Pigeon River.

The trail ascends along gushing Road Prong. After the third bridge on that stream, head right (west) at the junction, where the Road Prong Trail continues left (south) up the watershed (described in the Option below). Not far above the turn, the trail stands steeply up, with no switchbacks, confined in a tight ramp toward the ridge crest of Sugarland Mountain. As the trail veers right (north), the grade becomes more gradual, then dips to the apex of the ridge that leads to where the Chimneys rise into the sky.

The last climb is a rocky, low-grade scramble up the crags. Rock jocks may be comfortable with the first route straight up the pinnacle, but a warning sign urges the less adventurous (less foolhardy?) around the right side for an easier but still exciting climb to the rocky summit.

Savor the vista—among the best in the Smokies. To start, this is a summit perch as iconic as you're likely to find anywhere—and you've earned it! To the northwest, the Sugarlands Valley plummets to Gatlinburg. Northeast, the squiggle of The Loop in the Newfound Gap Road lies below. Far above, Mount LeConte shows off all four of its named summits.

The horizon begs to be scanned. Consider taking a topo map of the park and a compass on this hike. Correctly orient the open map by turning it until north on the compass and on the compass rose of the map match. Then aim the compass at landmarks on the horizon—but keep the dial aligned with north on the map—and when you place the compass down on Chimney Tops, it should be pointing to the spot on the horizon you're trying to identify. The Smokies is a wealth of opportunities for this kind of fun (for more, check out FalconGuides' *Route Finding*).

Option

If you'd like to see a lofty, more defined section of the old road across the Smokies like the Sugarlands Valley Self-Guiding Nature Trail, follow the Chimney Tops Trail for 0.9 mile, and where that trail turns right (west), follow the Road Prong Trail left (south) as far as you care to walk. This historic old Native American trail, said to be the oldest in the park, has seen centuries of travel on its rise to and across Indian Gap.

The trail was upgraded to road status in the 1830s and was the only road over the Smokies until the 1920s, when the Newfound Gap Road was built. Indian Gap was once thought to be the Smokies' lowest gap, until Professor Arnold Guyot determined that to be Newfound Gap, hence the change in the road crossing. The road saw a lot of activity in the Civil War, including improvements by a force made up of many Cherokee Indians and led by Colonel William H. Thomas, a white man raised as a Cherokee who would later become the tribe's chief.

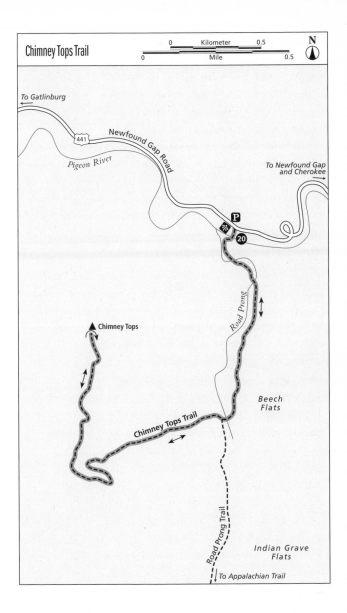

Chimney Tops Trail

| 0 | Kilometer | 0.5 |
| 0 | Mile | 0.5 |

N

To Gatlinburg

441 Newfound Gap Road

Pigeon River

To Newfound Gap
and Cherokee

P

20

Road Prong

Chimney Tops

Chimney Tops Trail

Beech
Flats

Road Prong Trail

Indian Grave
Flats

To Appalachian Trail

Just 0.3 mile above the divergence of the Chimney Tops and Road Prong Trails, you'll reach Indian Grave Flats, the burial site of a Cherokee guide killed by Union raiders. Just 0.1 mile above that, there's a tricky stream crossing at Standing Rock Ford (you won't miss the standing rock). About 0.5 mile above is Talking Falls.

The trail becomes rougher as it reaches the crest of the ridge and dips over to the Clingmans Dome Road, 2.4 miles from the turnoff to Chimney Tops. For those who want to wander one way down the trail, you can spot a car or arrange a shuttle between the Chimney Tops Trail parking area and the Road Prong Trail at the Indian Gap Parking Area, located 1.2 miles from Newfound Gap on Clingmans Dome Road.

Miles and Directions

0.0 Start from the parking area.

0.1 Cross the first bridge over Walker Camp Prong.

0.4 Cross the second bridge over Road Prong.

0.8 Cross the third bridge over Road Prong.

0.9 At the Road Prong Trail junction, stay right (west) on the Chimney Tops Trail.

2.0 Reach the Chimney Tops summit. This is the turnaround point.

4.0 Arrive back at the trailhead.

21 Elkmont Self-Guiding Nature Trail

This is one of the best of the nature trails in the park that focuses on the changing Smokies' landscape. The path and accompanying brochure do a good job of pointing out the clues to where human activity has disturbed the forest, and of explaining how nature is responding.

Distance: 0.8-mile loop

Approximate hiking time: 45 minutes

Difficulty: Easy

Trail surface: Stable forest trail with a very rooty section at the top of the path

Other trail users: None; no dogs or horses allowed

Best season: Spring for wildflowers, and late summer for profuse mushrooms

Canine compatibility: Dogs not permitted

Fees and permits: None

Schedule: Adjacent Elkmont Campground is open year-round.

Maps: USGS Gatlinburg; TOPO! North Carolina, South Carolina

Trail contacts: Information about trails, camping, road closures, as well as downloadable maps and a "Smokies Trip Planner" are available online under the "Plan Your Visit" part of the park's excellent Web site, www .nps.gov/grsm. The Backcountry Information Office is open 9 a.m. to noon, 865-436-1297.

Special considerations: For campers in the Elkmont Campground's A through F sites, a side trail leads to the nature trail between sites C11 and C12. Restrooms are located just across from those sites, making them accessible from the Nature Trail.

Finding the trailhead: Turn onto Little River Road at Sugarlands Visitor Center, and drive 4.9 miles to a left (south) turn toward Elkmont Campground. Bear left (east) past the campground entrance at 6.3 miles, and turn left (east) into the nature trail parking area at 6.7 miles. GPS: N35 39.459' / W83 34.834'

The Hike

The Elkmont Campground area was the site of a major logging operation in the early twentieth century. A logging railroad from Townsend, Tennessee, reached through this area to the heart of the Smokies. The extensive timbering that occurred largely clear-cut the forests, and the trail shows how the wholesale removal of trees has determined where different species have come to dominate in settings that offer them more or less ideal conditions for growth.

The trail leaves the parking area to the right (east). You'll notice what appears to be an old foundation near post #1. Cross a single log bridge with asphalt tread to aid your grip. You can't miss the old logging railroad that the trail follows past posts #2 and #3 before it veers away to the right. A mossy scenic seep appears past posts #4 and #5, where an old spring box sits beside the trail. In this area you'll be amazed by a poplar to the left of the trail that's been explosively shattered by lightning. Speaking of forest products—here's a lifetime supply of toothpicks.

At post #6, a side trail wanders left (northwest) of the main trail along the little stream, and then rejoins the formal path as you cross a single log span and start your rise out the drainage at about 0.2 mile. Notice how the trail rises into a richly aromatic understory of rhododendron and mountain laurel, with galax beneath. At about 0.3 mile the trail crests as it passes a few benches on a very rooty tread that might give the unsure of foot a second thought.

A sharp left turn takes you down toward the parking lot. Just above your car, be sure to follow the zigzag of reinforced switchbacks designed to prevent erosion and bootleg routes that had developed on this side of the parking area.

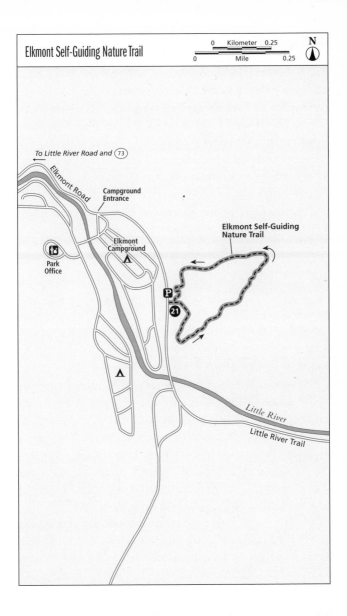

Elkmont Self-Guiding Nature Trail

0   Kilometer   0.25

0   Mile   0.25

N

To Little River Road and (73)

Elkmont Road

Campground Entrance

Elkmont Campground

Park Office

Elkmont Self-Guiding Nature Trail

P

21

Little River

Little River Trail

Miles and Directions

0.0 Start to the right (east), passing post #1 and crossing a log bridge.

0.2 Rise out of the drainage.

0.3 The pathway is pretty rooty across this high point of the trail.

0.8 Arrive back at the trailhead.

22 Abrams Falls

This dramatic waterfall—the park's biggest by volume of water—leaps off a ledge into a misty plunge pool. Tackle this trail after significant rain and you'll be impressed.

Distance: 5 miles out and back
Approximate hiking time: 3 to 4 hours
Difficulty: Moderate
Trail surface: Packed earth, but with some rocky, stony sections
Other trail users: None; no dogs or horses allowed
Best season: Spring, after rainfall, and during off-times (such as weekdays) to escape the crowds
Canine compatibility: Dogs not permitted
Fees and permits: None
Schedule: Cades Cove Loop Road is open sunrise to sunset, 7 days a week, year–round. Between early May and late September, it is closed Wednesday and Sunday mornings till 10 a.m. for use by pedestrians and bicyclists.
Maps: USGS Calderwood and Cades Cove; TOPO! Tennessee, Kentucky
Trail contacts: Information about trails, camping, road closures, as well as downloadable maps and a "Smokies Trip Planner" are available online under the "Plan Your Visit" part of the park's excellent Web site, www .nps.gov/grsm. The Backcountry Information Office is open 9 a.m. to noon, 865-436-1297.
Special considerations: The 11-mile loop of Cades Cove—one of the park's best motor tours—is justifiably popular for its outstanding scenery (a pristine rural valley surrounded by summits) and great interpretation of early Smokies' residents. Pick up the Cades Cove Tour booklet from the roadside information kiosk at the start of the loop. At all but off-times and seasons, or in inclement weather, this can be a slow crawl of motorists stopping to ogle deer and bears, etc. Do everyone a favor—do not stop in the road for any reason. If you want to look, at least pull off or

out of the way so the traffic flow will not be impeded.

Other: If this hike is too much for you, start at the Abrams Falls trailhead, but turn right (north), across the bridge, and make an easy 1-mile out-and-back hike to the Elijah Oliver Place. Notice the "stranger room" added onto the front porch, a feature you'll also see at the Dan Lawson Place farther along the loop. Or consider the new Pine Oak Nature Trail in the Cades Cove Campground, a tree identification trail reopened with the recent decision to no longer maintain the Cades Cove Self-Guiding Nature Trail (located on the loop road 0.4 past the Cable Mill Historic Area and visitor center on the right/west).

Finding the trailhead: From the US 321/TN 73 intersection in Townsend, drive 2.3 miles into the park and go right (southwest) onto the Laurel Creek Road at the junction where TN 73 continues left (east) as the Little River Road to (and from) Sugarlands Visitor Center. Measuring from this junction, the campground/picnic area (where restrooms are available at the nearby camp store) and the start of the Cades Cove motor loop is at 7.5 miles. At 5.1 miles from the campground, turn right (west) onto the 0.5-mile access road to the trailhead. GPS: N35 35.467' / W83 51.032'

The Hike

Cross the bridge to start the hike, and the trail wanders streamside on a rocky, stony tread. It then climbs moderately to a crest, and dips into a beautiful dark forest of bigger trees. Now on a packed earth path, you'll dip back down to the stream—the first of three times the route will climb into the quiet well above the rushing sounds of Abrams Creek, and then return.

You'll wander along the level streamside for a significant distance after the first hump, crossing a single-log bridge, with trailside views of the creek. Then you'll rise again, more steeply now, on a packed tread into a drier pine forest past significant signs of a forest fire (a controlled burn conducted around 2006). At the top the trail slips through the craggy crest of Arbutus Ridge on a shelf hewn from the rock.

Past the ridge the trail jogs into a really beautiful spot—a sharply benched trail along a rock outcropping with many kinds of wildflowers. Heading down again, the route returns to parallel the stream. Travel a second long flat stretch, where the creek suddenly dances to life over beautiful ledges. A second log bridge crosses a rocky sluice and you pass through towering, evenly spaced trees in an open forest (more evidence of fire—this one part of a backfire set to combat a blaze started by lightning). Then you'll climb again, as does the river, but you are above it as it weaves in and around ridges into drier woods with more evidence of fire.

At a sign warning against climbing near the falls (and urging parents to carefully control children), Abrams Falls is immediately below but not visible. The trail turns right (north), descends to cross another bridge over a side stream, then follows that stream left (west) to a junction on the bank of Abrams Creek. Abrams Falls Trail continues to the right (north) along the stream, but go left (south), back across the side stream on another bridge to the base of the falls.

The sign at the streamside junction (and another back at the trailhead) warns that a handful of people have drowned in the swirling currents at the base of this thundering cataract (a word to the wise!). A ledge provides safe access along the base of the cliff to the edge of the cascade (but use caution—don't get too close). The Cherokee name for Cades Cove, *Tsiyahi,* means place of the otter. Keep your

Abrams Falls

eyes peeled—you might be lucky and glimpse a river otter. More than 300 were released in the Smokies in 1984 and they often cavort in the pool.

Miles and Directions

0.0 Start from the parking area at the end of the gravel access road.

0.1 Go left across the bridge.

1.0 Cross Arbutus Ridge.

2.1 Pass the waterfall warning sign at the crest of the ridge.

2.4 Go left (south) at the streamside junction and the second warning sign about drownings.

2.5 Reach the base of the falls.

5.0 Arrive back at the trailhead.

About the Author

Randy Johnson is a widely published authority on the Appalachian outdoors. He's the author of the best-selling guidebooks *Hiking North Carolina, Hiking the Blue Ridge Parkway* (both FalconGuides), and many others. Articles and photos by this award-winning photojournalist have for decades brought the Appalachians to readers of national magazines, newspapers, and major outdoor Web sites. As editor of the country's most award-winning airline magazine, he often focused on accessible adventure. A trail designer and builder, Randy was the founding wilderness manager at Grandfather Mountain and helped ensure the preservation of this significant North Carolina summit as a United Nations–designated biosphere reserve, and now a state park. He was a trail design consultant for the Blue Ridge Parkway's Tanawha Trail and worked to mesh Grandfather Mountain's then-private trails and Park Service paths into the system in place today. He's a longtime resident of the North Carolina mountains and lives in Banner Elk. Visit www.randyjohnsonbooks.com to check out his television and radio appearances, videos, publications, and more.